Cristina Davino · Luigi Fabbris
Editors

Survey Data Collection and Integration

W0006190

 Springer

Editors
Cristina Davino
Department of Studies for Economic
    Development
University of Macerata
Macerata
Italy

Luigi Fabbris
Department of Statistical Science
University of Padua
Padua
Italy

ISBN 978-3-642-21307-6   ISBN 978-3-642-21308-3   (eBook)
DOI 10.1007/978-3-642-21308-3
Springer Heidelberg New York Dordrecht London

Library of Congress Control Number: 2012943361

Printed on acid-free paper

Springer is part of Springer Science+Business Media (www.springer.com)

Preface

Surveys are an important source of scientific knowledge and a valid decision-support tool in many fields, from social studies to economics, market research, health studies, and others. Scientists have investigated most of the methodological issues on statistical surveys so that the scientific literature offers excellent references concerning all the required steps for planning and realising surveys. Nevertheless, real problems of statistical surveys often require practical solutions that either deviate from the consolidated methodology or do not have a specific solution at all.

Information and communication technology and techniques are earmarking the modern world, changing people's behavior and mentality. Innovations in remote and wireless communication devices are being created at full steam. Purchase behaviors, service fruition, production activities, social and natural events are recorded in real time and stored in huge data warehouses. Warehouses are being created not only for data but also for textual documents, audio files, images, and video files. Survey methods must evolve accordingly: surveys have to take advantage of all new information chances and adapt, if needed, the basic methodology to the ways people use to communicate, memorize, and screen the information. This book is aimed at focusing on new topics in today's survey researchers' agenda.

Let us provide an example of new survey needs. Complex survey designs, which were imagined as statistical means for collecting data from samples of dwellings drawn from population registers, are going to be obsolete but for some official statistics and for rare, relevant, opinion surveys. In fact, the access to population registers has proven strict and face-to-face interviewing has become very expensive. Instead, there are growing possibilities for both private and public organisation for achieving administrative databases related to large population segments. Hence, sample surveys are on the verge of specialisation in collecting subjective information through remote technological devices from samples mechanically drawn from available databases. Our vision is purposively drastic because we want to stress the irreversibility of the trend.

Any survey researcher has to ponder practical and methodological problems when choosing the appropriate technique for acquiring the data to analyse. No researcher is allowed to ignore costs, time, and organisation constraints of data collection. See also the introductory paper by Luigi Biggeri on this issue. This induces a researcher to consider appropriate for her/his purposes:

- Integrating large datasets from various sources rather than gathering ad hoc data by means of traditional surveys;
- Collecting low-cost, real-time massive data rather than gathering data through refined statistical techniques at the expenses of timeliness, budget saving, and respondent bothering;
- Estimating some parameters without sampling error, because all units can be processed, and other parameters based on models that hypothesize at the very local level relationships that are observed at a higher scale, as in the case of small area estimation;
- Connecting and harmonising in a holistic approach, data collected with or analysed at different scales, for instance analyse together data on individual graduates, graduates' families, professors, study programmes, educational institutions, production companies, and local authorities, all aimed at describing the complex (i.e. multidimensional and hierarchical) relationships between graduates' education and work.

Of course, we go nowhere if our research aims are unclear. Supposing aims are clear, then the appropriateness of research choices is a methodological concern. In this volume, a paper by Tomàs Aluja-Banet, Josep Daunis-i-Estadella, and Yan Hong Chen, as well as another by Diego Bellisai, Stefania Fivizzani, and Marina Sorrentino concern the issue of data integration. The first paper deals with the issues to be considered when imputing, in place of a missing value, values drawn from related sources. It deals also with the choice of an imputation model and with the possibility to combine parametric and non-parametric imputation models. The second paper applies to the design of an official survey aimed at integrating data collected on job vacancy and hours worked with other Istat business surveys. A third paper by Monica Pratesi, Caterina Giusti, and Stefano Marchetti discusses the use of small area estimation methods to measure the incidence of poverty at the sub-regional level using EU-SILC sample data.

The very availability of large databases requires researchers to focus on data quality. We mean that data quality assessment is an important issue in any survey, but it tends to the fore just because the sampling error vanishes. This, in turn, requires researchers to learn:

- How to check the likelihood of the data drawn from massive databases whose records could contain errors?
- How to measure the quality of, and possibly adjust, the data collected with opinion surveys that, in general, are carried out by means of high-performance technological tools and by specialized personnel who interview samples of respondents?

- How to guarantee sufficient methodological standards in data collection from key witnesses whom applied researchers turn to more and more often so to corroborate the results of analyses on inaccessible phenomena, to elicit people's preferences or hidden behaviors and to forecast social or economical events in the medium or the long run?
- How to prune the redundant information that concurrent databases and repetitive records contain? Also, how to screen the statistically valid from the coarse information in excessively loaded databases created for purposes that are alien to statistics?

This is the reason why, in this volume, methodologies for measuring statistical errors and for designing complex questionnaires are picked out. Statistical errors refer to both sampling and non-sampling errors. The paper by Giovanni D' Alessio and Giuseppe Ilardi examines methods for measuring the effects of non-response errors ("unit non-response") and of some response errors ("uncorrelated measurement errors" and "biases from underreporting") by taking advantage of the experience from the Bank of Italy's Survey on Household Income and Wealth. The Authors suggest, too, how to overcome the error effects on estimates through various techniques and models and by means of auxiliary information.

Questionnaire design and question wording instructions, as strategies for preventing data collection errors, are dealt with extensively in the volume. Cristina Davino and Rosaria Romano discuss the case of multi-item scales that are appropriate for the measurement of subjective data, focussing on how individual propensities in the use of scales can be interpreted, in particular within strata of respondents. Luigi Fabbris covers the presentation of batteries of interrelated items for scoring or ranking sets of choice or preference items. Five types of item presentations in questionnaires are crossed with potential estimation models and computer-assisted data collection modes. Caterina Arcidiacono and Immacolata Di Napoli present and apply the so-called Cantril scale that self-anchors the extremes of a scale and is useful in psychological research. Simona Balbi and Nicole Triunfo deal with the age-old problem of closed- and open-ended questions, in the perspective of statistical analysis of data. The Authors tackle, in particular, the problem of transforming textual data, i.e. data that are collected in natural language, into data that can be processed with multivariate statistical methods.

This volume is a consequence of the stimulating debate that animated the workshop "Thinking about methodology and applications of surveys" that took place at the University of Macerata (Italy) in September 2010. The titles of the papers presented in the volume have been proposed to the Authors having in mind the relevant issues of a homogeneous field of study that is usually covered by undirected articles. In each paper, a survey of the scientific literature is discussed and remarks and innovative solutions to face today's survey problems are suggested. All papers aim at balancing formal rigour with simplicity of the presentation style so as to address the book both to practitioners involved in applied survey research and to academics interested in scientific development of surveys.

The editors of the volume like to highlight that all papers have been referred by at least two external experts in the topical field. The editors wish to thank the Authors and also the Referees for their invaluable contribution to the quality of the papers. The external referees involved were: Giorgio Alleva (University of Rome "La Sapienza", Italy), Gianni Betti (University of Siena, Italy), Silvia Biffignandi (University of Bergamo, Italy), Sergio Bolasco (University of Rome "La Sapienza", Italy), Marisa Civardi (Bicocca University in Milan, Italy), Daniela Cocchi (University of Bologna, Italy), Giuseppe Giordano (University of Salerno, Italy), Michael Greenacre (Universitat Pompeu Fabra, Barcelona, Spain), Filomena Maggino (University of Florence, Italy), Alberto Marradi (University of Florence, Italy), Giovanna Nicolini (University of Milan, Italy), Maria Francesca Romano (Scuola Superiore Sant'Anna, Italy).

The editors are open to any contribution of readers who would wish to comment on papers or to propose the Authors other ideas.

Cristina Davino
Luigi Fabbris

Contents

Part I
Introduction to Statistical Surveys

Surveys: Critical Points, Challenges and Need for Development

Luigi Biggeri

Abstract The aim of this paper is to review some of the critical issues which need further insight in survey methodology and practice. The focus is on the specific aspects of the survey process grouping the main issues in the following three areas: (i) mode of collection of data and construct of questionnaire; (ii) sampling strategy, design and estimation, to reply to the demands of the users and integration of data; (iii) data dissemination and standardisation. For every issue survey data producers have to fight and ask for development.

1 Introduction

Statistical survey methodology and applications—from the data collection to the dissemination of the results—have improved greatly during the last decades but the discussions in this field are still to the fore in international and national statistical research and in statistical scientific congresses. For example, three scientific events in this field were organized recently in Italy: in 2007, a Satellite conference of the International Association of Survey Statisticians (IASS) on "Small Area Estimation" was held in Pisa (SAE2007), in 2009, the "First Italian Conference on Survey Methodology" took place in Siena (ITACOSM09) and in 2010 a Workshop on "Statistical Surveys: thinking about methodology and applications" was organized in Macerata (SS2010). However, various issues, concerning both the methodology and practice of statistical surveys, still require discussion and improvement; in particular, operative solutions for them must be defined.

The aim of this paper is to review some of the critical issues which need development on the producer side. The presentation of the paper is organized as follows.

L. Biggeri (✉)
Department of Statistics, University of Florence,
Florence, Italy
e-mail: biggeri@ds.unifi.it

C. Davino and L. Fabbris (eds.), *Survey Data Collection and Integration*,
DOI: 10.1007/978-3-642-21308-3_1, © Springer-Verlag Berlin Heidelberg 2013

Section 2 presents some frameworks regarding the relationship between users and producers of survey data and the life cycle of a survey - from the design, data producer and quality assessment perspectives.. The frameworks will allow us to focus on the specific aspects of the survey process that still present critical issues, which will be discussed in Sect. 3 together with the challenges and the need for development of research topics in this field. Some concluding remarks are presented in Sect. 4.

2 Frameworks to Specify and Organize the Presentation of the Critical Issues of Statistical Surveys

Statistical surveys are not the only method for collecting information about the population (i.e., there are administrative record systems, qualitative investigations, observation of the behaviour of persons, randomised experiments, etc.). However, we focus on survey methodology and practice seeking to identify principles about the design, collection, processing and analysis of survey data that are linked to the cost and quality of survey estimates.

The production processes and 'quality' of survey data can be defined within two main frameworks, labelled: (i) *Total Quality Management*, and (ii) *Total Survey Error paradigm*. These frameworks are useful for identifying the areas of the critical issues that may need development.

2.1 The Total Quality Management Approach

Since the 1990s, scholars have debated the possibility of referring to the Total Quality Management (TQM) approach for producing statistical information and improving its quality (Groves 1989; Groves and Tortora 1991; U.S. Bureau of Labor Statistics 1994). What we would like to stress from the outset is the importance of discussing the improvement of the quality of statistical survey results, not only as regards checking and evaluating possible sampling and non-sampling errors, but also as an approach to their construction and computation, including continuous checking and revision of the design of their production process to satisfy the *users' needs*.

Therefore, in general, and in order to decide (by systematic evaluation) which kind of improvements in the statistical measures are necessary and feasible, it is necessary to follow a Total Quality Measurement Model which, at least in part, may be similar to an experimental design in Taguchi's approach, in order to evaluate the importance of the different methods which are used in the survey and may affect its results.

A simplified framework of the TQM referred to the production of statistical measures is reported in the following Fig. 1.

It is evident from the framework that the starting point for organising a survey and producing statistical measures is the information requirements of the users.

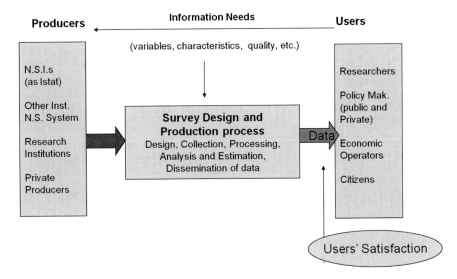

Fig. 1 Total quality management framework for a statistical survey

Three important characteristics of the current production of statistical measures are: (i) the organisation of statistical production must be *user oriented*, looking for the optimisation of the users' satisfaction; (ii) the *emphasis* is placed *on the quality* of all statistical information produced, which is given increasing attention to the check of users' satisfaction; (iii) the resources available for statistical production are scarce, and in any case it is very important to take into account the cost of the survey (*cost constraints*).

The information needs must be specified in terms of variables of interest with their characteristics and, above all, in terms of the quality characteristics of the survey result (of the survey statistics (y)).

With regard to the inputs or process variables (factors), it can be said, in general, that some of them are controllable factors, while other inputs can be considered uncontrollable (or noise) factors; i.e. environmental factors. For an example of application of the framework for the calculation of price indices, see Fig. 2.

In theory, a quality-cost model or cost-error model should serve as a mechanism for evaluating the performance of a statistical measure, insuring good statistical measures while balancing cost and costumer satisfaction. The model could be used to evaluate the cost of alternative designs and to balance each alternative contribution against the analytical goals of the programme. This means that the field focuses on improving quality within cost constraints or, alternatively, reducing costs for a given level of quality.

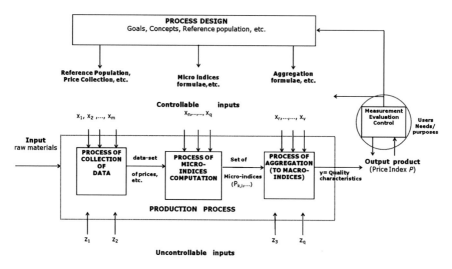

Fig. 2 A simplified production process for price indices

2.2 The Production Process of a Survey: Different Perspectives of the Life Cycle of a Survey

It is well known that the design and the realisation of a survey production process can be presented in a structured manner, as an explosion of the central box of Figure 1, using the three different perspectives of the *Life Cycle of a Survey* taken according to Groves et al. (2009) and presented in Figs. 3, 4 and 5. The frameworks refer to a sample survey, but it can be easily extended to a complete survey as well. It is also obvious that the subsequent phases indicated in the frameworks are often overlapping and influence each other, taking on precise shapes only with reference to a concrete case.

The *design perspective* of the life cycle of a survey shows that it moves from abstract ideas to execution and concrete actions. Figure 3 shows that there are two parallel aspects of surveys: the description of a target population and of population attributes and the measurement of construct. The representational dimension concerns which population(s) should be described by the survey (as requested by the users), meanwhile the measurement process describes what data are to be collected concerning the observational units in the survey. Without a good survey design, it is quite difficult to obtain good survey statistics; therefore, each phase must be designed carefully.

Figure 4 shows how a survey design becomes a process from the *producer's perspective*, indicating the steps for developing a survey, starting from the definition of the research (survey) objectives. There are two main lines of decisions: one regarding the sample and another regarding the measurement process (where the measurement instruments are shaped). The preparation of the data file to be used for estimation

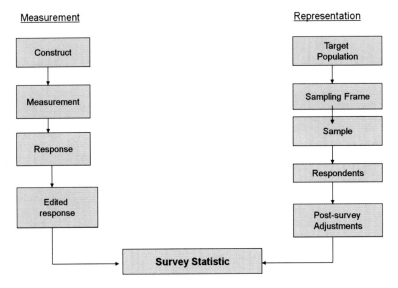

Fig. 3 The life cycle of a survey from a design perspective

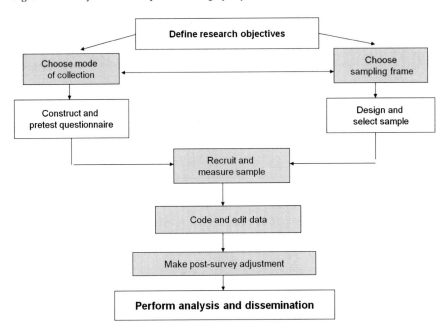

Fig. 4 A survey from a producer process perspective

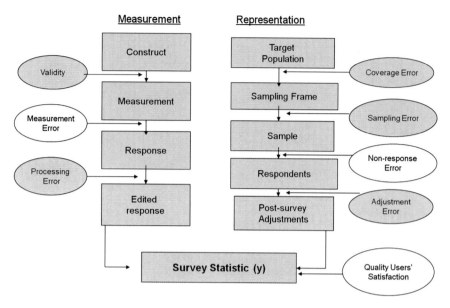

Fig. 5 The life cycle of a survey from a quality perspective

or analysis often undergoes some post-survey adjustments, mainly for coverage and non-response errors.

In order to judge the quality of data obtained with a survey, it is necessary to estimate the possible errors that might incur during the implementation of the survey. The *quality perspective* of the survey life cycle, shown in Fig. 5, indicates a set of quality concepts that are common in survey methodology (this framework is sometimes labelled the 'Total survey error paradigm'). Because the quality is an attribute not of the survey but of individual statistics, its shape obviously depends on the statistics considered. The ovals of Fig. 5 contain the word 'error' with reference to the type of error commonly defined. The validity, indicated as an issue between construct and measurement phases, is the extent to which the measures reflect the underlying construct.

From the presentation of the frameworks, it is clear that the needs and the request of the users affect all the production process of the survey and that all the phases of the survey and the decisions of the producer depend on the purpose of the survey. Moreover, the subsequent phases are often overlapping and influence each other, taking precise shapes for the related operations only with reference to a concrete case.

Wishing to specify the current critical issues of the statistical surveys, both methodological and practical, it is opportune to refer to the different phases and errors mentioned in the previous frameworks. In this way, each issue can be located in terms of request coming from users or from research results and in terms of its effect on the phases of three life cycles of survey perspectives (design, production process and quality assessment).

3 Critical Issues, Challenges and Need for Development of Statistical Surveys

3.1 Why are There Still Critical Issues?

Some critical issues, both methodological and practical, arise from various researches, but important issues also derive from *new requests from the users*. In fact, users are asking for:

- more variables and multiple characteristics for each target population;
- more detailed data at territorial level (for small areas) and for linked succession of events for environmental analyses in particular;
- data for rare populations;
- data for difficult-to-reach populations;
- data for longitudinal studies;
- more timely data, in the field of short term indicators;
- trustworthy dissemination of data (i.e. satisfying the principles of official statistics data must be impartial, reliable, consistent, cost-effective, easy to interpret, with the guarantee of confidentiality);
- full transparency of the measured concepts, data and methods underlying the compilation of these data, and the use of the same definitions for the same target population measured with different surveys.

Most of the issues affect the target population and the objectives of the surveys, and consequently affect all the phases of the surveys and, in particular, the methods for sampling design and estimation. The latter two issues refer to the dissemination phase, but also affect the measurement construct and design.

On the other hand, many researches carried out by both official and academic statisticians have given rise to the need for focusing more attention to several other issues, some of them are perennial problems, regarding the following aspects:

- integration of modes of data collection for improving cost-efficiency of the collection process and the quality of data collected;
- use of open-ended questions;
- order effect of questions mainly in opinion survey;
- interpretation of the responses in the questionnaire, particularly the subjective and self-assessed responses;
- interviewer falsification;
- analysis of non-responses;
- analysis of selection biases;
- use of web surveys;

- use of non-probabilistic samples, particularly important in opinion surveys;
- integration of competing surveys.

Therefore, survey producers have to face many challenges, taking into account the cost constraints (available resources) and efficiency as well as the need for flexibility and adaptability of survey design and organisation.

We will focus only on some aspects of the life cycle of a survey that seem to us more interesting, that is:

1. Mode of collection of data and construct of questionnaire (Sect. 3.2);
2. Sampling design and error estimation, to reply to the demands of the users; and integration of data-collection modes (Sect. 3.3);
3. Dissemination of data and standardisation (Sect. 3.4).

Below is a summary of the characteristics of the critical issues and some recent developments.[1]

3.2 Mode of Collection of Data and Construct of a Questionnaire

To reply to the new demands of users and to improve cost-efficiency of data collection and data quality, the producers of surveys are modifying and *integrating the different modes of collection of data*. Methods for exploiting and combining existing and new data sources (e.g. administrative registers, traditional surveys, electronic traces, Internet information, etc., require more attention to the construct of the questionnaires, mode of data collection and respondent burden).

In particular, producers of statistics are using more and more the *web* as a mode of data collection (Tourangeau et al. 2009). The reasons for offering a web alternative lie in data quality and cost considerations. However the proportion of respondents to the web surveys is low, and to mixed-mode mail and web surveys as well. In the latter case, the respondents are inclined to select the mode that is immediately at hand.

Whatever the case, it is necessary to cope with the problem of *decreasing response rates* in surveys (Yan et al. 2010; de Heer 1999), and implement the *imputation and estimation methods* under non-ignorable non-responses (De Leeuw et al. 2003; Graham and Olchowski 2007), that cause serious problems in any survey and in particular in longitudinal studies (Razafindratsima and Sarter 2008).

Recently, some experiments have been implemented at Statistics Sweden in mixed-mode mail and web surveys (Holmberg et al. 2010). The use of alternative strategies pointed out that the most 'web-intensive' alternative strategy is showing

---

[1] Usually, we do not refer to the methods and application to a specific economic and/or social field. However, we would like to mention the important developments that have been achieved and discussed during the International Conferences on Establishment Surveys. A special section of the Journal of Official Statistics (Atkinson et al. 2010) has been devoted to host part of the papers presented at the Third Conference on Establishment Surveys

potential for considerable increase in the proportion of responses completed through the web mode. A cost reduction can also be expected using the 'web-intensive' strategies.

Hence, the use of the web survey mode requires paying attention to the *selection bias*, which has been studied at length also for other modes of data collection; also using voluntary participation for example, which is frequent in private and opinion surveys. The problem was studied recently by Schonlau et al. (2006) and was solved using propensity scores. Finally, we maintain that the effect of the web survey mode on data quality necessitates further checking.

Another group of problems, only new in part, refers to the organisation of question-naires and to the interpretation of the reply to *subjective* and *open-ended questions*, and to interviewer falsification of data.

The self-reported data and subjective replies usually prevent comparability across socio-economic groups and countries. Moreover, social researchers working with surveys often face the difficulty that the concept they are interested in cannot be objectively measured. Measurement problems lead to individual heterogeneity in the interpretation of the survey questions and to the incomparability between respondent answers. This is usually known as 'differential item functioning' (DIF). DIF is often ignored and the variable collected is treated as a questionnaire variable, which may lead to misleading results (for example, student's replies on a qualitative scale for assessing the quality of teaching).

A new approach and powerful tool to enhance the problem is the use of 'anchoring vignettes', as advocated by King et al. (2004) and generalised by King and Wand (2007) and also by Hopkins and King (2010). Anchoring vignettes are one of the solutions and are particular versions of questionnaires that are used to achieve a DIF, introducing the idea that, under a specific hypothesis, an individual's self-assessment can be rescaled by using the answers to a set of vignettes that reflect the situation of hypothetical people.

The question wording and the classifications of replies, even on the same subject, differ in different surveys and, above all, the use of different scales in the reply is one of the main issues for the interpretation and comparison of collected data, even for the same target population and survey objective.

One dilemma facing survey designers concerns the use of *open-ended questions* to improve the quality of information. However, open-ended questions have a reputation for poor-quality responses, difficulty in coding, and costly administration. In addition, survey designers often need to fit items within the constraint of a page-limit, so open-ended questions are often either reduced into allocated spaces or eliminated outright, and using such questions has proven problematic especially in mail surveys. But, *open-ended questions* have the potential to generate rich, detailed answers and can provide valuable information to understand the replies and to help researchers to understand a respondent's thinking. Thus, there is a need to examine how and when open-ended questions can be used in mail surveys. Survey results are influenced by visual design components as well as by question wording and the offer of response options.

Recently, Israel (2010) used experimental data to assess the impact of the amount of space offered for the answers on the length and content of responses to two open-ended questions. The results of the analysis suggest that it is better to design larger spaces for the answers to fully capture high-quality responses.

Finally, the *interviewer falsification* of data is an important issue, particularly for opinion surveys and private data producers. For this reason, some associations (for example the American Association for Public Opinion Research - AAPOR) organised specific meetings and prepared a report on the status (practices and policies) of interviewer falsification. There are many methods for detecting interviewer falsification and some researchers propose to do it by including the use of data mining (Murphy et al. 2005).

3.3 Sampling Design and Estimation that Reply to the Demands of the Users

The new requests made by the users for more variables and multiple characteristics of interest for each target population and for more detailed and timely data, require the survey producers to reply to the new challenges by implementing multi-products and multi-purpose surveys and small area estimation, integrating more than one source of data coming from different sample surveys and/or administrative archives and giving new attention to the sampling strategy.

(a) One important methodological challenge is the implementation of multi-products and multi-domain surveys, when overall sample size is bounded.

  The use of information on population(s) under study for the efficient design of surveys has been studied extensively. Well-known methods for efficient sample design include stratification and probability proportional to size. However, these methods are designed to select efficient samples when there is only one survey characteristic of interest. In order to select *efficient samples when there are multiple characteristics of interest*, the traditional method of stratification is not sufficient if the characteristics are not well correlated among them, and is usually carried out without considering the optimisation problem of sampling size and allocation.

  Besides, when the stratified sample is used and the strata are obtained through cross classification of variables, the number of strata can be larger than the overall sample size.

  In these cases, an optimal stratification of a sampling frame can be determined together with optimal sampling size and allocation of units in strata (Ballin and Barcaroli 2008). However, some limitations are still affecting the proposed methods and additional work is required to overcome this.

  Also, the use of the balanced sampling technique and a greg-type estimation is proposed by Falorsi and Righi (2008). The proposal may be extended easily to a strategy employing the use of both direct and indirect small area estimators.

Another method for selecting efficient samples when there are multiple characteristics of interest that are not necessarily well correlated, and where a set of design variables could be used for improving the efficiency of the sample design, is the *Cube sampling* proposed by Deville and Tillé (2004) and experimented by the Australian Bureau of Statistics (ABS, 2007). In the experiment, cube sampling achieves efficiency by selecting balanced samples on a set of design variables, taking into account that the ABS household surveys have a multistage stratified cluster sample design with selections undertaken typically in three stages: collection district, block and cluster. The results in the ABS paper suggest that cube sampling has the potential to provide significant savings in cost and therefore that further work in this area should be continued. This paper mentions other issues (e.g. variance estimation and rotation control) that would need to be considered before implementing cube sampling in the ABS.

(b) In the field of sample strategy and, above all, of the methods of estimation, the *small area estimation* is one of the survey topics most developed during recent years, also because these detailed data have proven useful for the analysis of local situations and for the implementation of socio-economic policies. In fact, many congresses and seminars have been organised and many methods of estimation have been proposed (SAE 2007; Chandra and Chambers 2009; Pratesi and Salvati 2009).

A contiguous topic is sampling spatial design and, in particular, sparse sampling, especially for measuring environmental problems and for analysing the events in the space (Dobbie et al. 2008) that present a review of approaches to spatial design.

Among the methods for detecting population units, particular attention is to be given now to innovative methods for surveying difficult-to-reach populations (Statistics Canada 2004).

In addition, the need for increased *timeliness of short-term data, especially in business statistics*, has become more pressing over recent years at both national and international level. In order to reply to the requests of the European institutions, preserving the accuracy of estimations, both OECD, Eurostat and national statistical organisations have established 'Short-term Economic Statistics Expert Groups'. A range of techniques can be applied for improving timeliness, reducing costs and/or improving accuracy.

Various approaches—re-design of sampling frame; focus on specific strata; panel samples; use of registers; introduction of approximations, etc,—to obtain estimates based on preliminary data are outlined (Werkhoven 2004; Falorsi et al. 2005), but because the request for anticipated estimates is increasing yet again, improved methods and experiments must be carried out.

(c) The *integration* and *calibration* of data is quite important to enlarge the information on target population, to connect repeated surveys in subsequent times and to verify the quality of the information collected (Verma et al. 2009). To achieve these objectives, calibration factors (that incorporate auxiliary data) can be used to adjust the sampling weights that make the estimates agree with the known totals (Kim and Park 2010; Särndal 2007). It might be that these kinds of methods could prove useful for improving non-probability and quota sampling as well. Moreover, the *'file concatenation'* approach can be used to integrate two (or more) sources of data which refer to the same target population (Ballin et al. 2008), and *embedded experiments* are often designed for the evaluation of changes in repeated and overlapping surveys when producers change the data collection methodology of their surveys to improve the efficiency of data collection and the quality of data in order to measure the effect of such a change on survey estimates under cost constraints (Chipperfield and Bell 2010).

The pooling of statistical information, coming both from sample surveys and/or archives is always difficult and obviously is one of the main problems we encounter when we have to struggle with probability-linked data (Chambers 2009). Moreover, challenges linked to the use of administrative registers are well known (both legally and methodologically) and a great deal of work is underway. The approach will depend on the varying conditions of single countries, including the legal basis (Zanutto and Zaslavsky 2002). One further challenge is also to establish (harmonised) quality criteria for registers and register-based statistics, and to define data quality indicators when combining survey data and administrative data.

3.4 Data Dissemination and Standardisation

When the data are collected and edited, their dissemination is the most important phase of the life cycle of a survey, in order to obtain the largest possible use of the data and to satisfy the user's needs.

The implementation of tools for data dissemination is continuously improving, taking into account the technological development of the media and Internet.

The users, and in particular the experts, are asking for *accurate* data, for clear information about their characteristics and quality (*transparency and metadata*) and for *access to elementary data* in order to carry out important research at the micro-level. Obviously, whatever the case, the respondents to the surveys have the right to the guarantee of their *privacy* (privacy *vs* accuracy). The legal framework and the methodological aspects of the issues mentioned are well developed and continue to be developed and applied, especially by national statistical institutes and international organisations (Couper et al. 2010).

Nowadays it is clear that there is dissemination of a very great amount of statistical data (also through Google), which frequently refers to the same target population with different results. The differences in these figures may arise from the different methods used to produce them, and the way statistical data are summarised or presented can lead to wrong conclusions even if the statistics are correct. But sometimes it seems that there is a kind of 'war of numbers', as the media say. Therefore, as statisticians, we must devote more attention to this aspect!

There is nothing more important than trustworthy statistics by the policy makers and the general public, not only for official statistics but also for private statistics.

The experts, the policy makers and the general public, must be put in a condition to trust official statistics and also private statistics; therefore, data producers should provide the best possible information on the economic and social phenomena.

However, statistics are the product of conscious choices: what to count and how to count. But choosing what and how to count, above all by private statistical producers, boils down to human judgment about the best way to get the answer to the question.

There are laws and statistical codes aiming at guaranteeing the impartiality and the quality of statistical data, in particular in the official statistics field (see for example, the codes for the European statistical system and for the Italian statistical system), and various codes of ethics defined by the associations of public opinion surveys and market surveys (see for example: the American Association of Public Opinion and Survey research professionals (AAPOR); but also ESOMAR, IPSOS, ASSIRM, etc). Private producers do not follow the rules every time and sometimes disseminate bad quality data. In Italy, the Authority for Communications has established rules for publishing and disseminating the results of opinion surveys in the media (actually, the survey methods followed, etc. are written in the Authority website, but the real work done by the survey team is not controlled).

The use of adequate methodologies and indicators means that the principles of impartiality, reliability, relevance, consistency, cost-effectiveness, statistical confidentiality and transparency are fully applied in official statistics but that is not enough.

The general public has not enough statistical knowledge to interpret statistical data and to evaluate the quality of data in order to understand if the available statistics are reliable or not, and frequently chooses data that confirm its ideas or do not trust statistics at all!

Actually, for this reason the statistical notion of quality is not useful for the general public. Statistical notion of the quality is not sufficient to achieve credibility, and consequently statisticians have to find other solutions to obtain credibility.

In our view, the only way to be successful in getting good data is to follow what has been done already in other (public) services: to be fully *transparent* on the concept of data and methods underlying the compilation of statistics and to implement *standardisation* of procedures, methods and presentation of the reports and *certification* of data and *accreditation* of the producers. It is not easy to follow this approach, but it is essential to do it.

Nowadays, the international and national organisations of official statistics and some international private associations of survey producers have already carried out and are currently doing some work in this field. Moreover, some statistical scientific associations are also operating in this sphere. Statistics Canada titled the 2011 International Methodological Symposium is 'Strategies for standardisation of methods and tools—How the get here', and obviously we must go ahead to try to get the awaited results for the general public being able to realise how reliable each statistic is.

4 Concluding Remarks

We have synthetically presented several issues and challenges that survey
producers have to face and which arise, as we have seen, from practical problems.
We cannot draw up a specific conclusion on the issue, but certainly we can state
that the most important aspect is the sample representativeness of the target population in web surveys and in non-probabilistic sampling surveys, that are carried out
frequently by private research bodies.

A great amount of work is currently underway and, obviously, it is necessary
to develop methods and experiments integrating the work of official and academic
statisticians. Fortunately, for a long time now this has been one of the distinctive
features of Italian scholars in statistics, and hopefully the involvement of private
professional statisticians as well will enhance the survey sector by establishing shared
views on data standardisation and certification.

References

Atkinson, A. D., Potter, F. J., Smith, P. A., Stettler, K., Willimack, D., & Yung, W. (guest Eds.).
    (2010). *Journal of Official Statistics, 26(1)* (Special Section with Articles Based on Papers from
    the Third International Conference on Establishment Surveys).
Ballin, M., & Barcaroli, G. (2008). Optimal stratification of sampling frames in a multivariate and
    multi domain sample design. *Contributi Istat, 10.*
Ballin, M., Di Zio, M., D'Orazio, M., Scanu, M., & Torelli, N. (2008). File concatenation of survey
    data: A computer intensive approach to sampling weights estimation (pp. 5–12). Roma: *Rivista
    di Statistica Ufficiale*, Istat.
Chambers, R. (2009). Regression analysis of probability-linked data. *Official Statistics Research
    Series, 4,* 1–72 (Statistics New Zealand).
Chandra, H., & Chambers, R. (2009). Multipurpose weighting for small area estimation. *Journal
    of Official Statistics, 25(3),* 379–395.
Chipperfield, J. (2007). *An evaluation of cube sampling for ABS household surveys.* Research
    Paper, Australian Bureau of Statistics, Camberra.
Chipperfield, J., & Bell, P. (2010). Embedded experiments in repeated and overlapping surveys.
    Journal of the Royal Statistical Society Series A, 51–56.
Couper, M. P., Singer, E., Conrad, F. G., & Groves, R. M. (2010). Experimental studies of disclosure
    risk, disclosure harm, topic sensitivity, and survey participation. *Journal of Official Statistics,
    26*(2), 287–300.
de Heer, W. (1999). International response trends: Results of an international survey. *Journal of
    Official Statistics, 15*(2), 129–142.
De Leeuw, E. D., Hox, J., & Huisman, M. (2003). Prevention and treatment of item nonresponse.
    Journal of Official Statistics, 19(2), 153–176.
Deville, J., & Tillé, Y. (2004). Efficient balanced sampling: The cube method. *Biometrika, 91,*
    893–912.
Dobbie, M. J., Henderson, B. L., & Stevens. D. L. (2008). Sparse sampling: Spatial design for
    monitoring stream networks. *Statistical Surveys, 2,* 113–153.
Falorsi, P., Alleva, G., Baccini, F., & Iannacone, R. (2005). Estimates based on preliminary data from
    a specific subsample and from respondents not included in the sub sample. *Statistical Methods
    and Applications, 4*(1), 83–99.

Falorsi, P. D., & Righi, P. (2008). A balanced sampling approach for multi-way stratification designs for small area estimation. *Contributi Istat*, *12*, 1–29.

Graham, J. W., & Olchowski, A. E. (2007). How many imputations are really needed? Some practical clarifications of multiple imputation theory. *Prevention Science Journal*, *8*(3), 206–213.

Groves, R. M. (1989). *Survey errors and survey costs*. New York: Wiley.

Groves, R. M., Fowler, F. J., Couper, M. P., Lepkowski, J. M., Singer, E., & Tourangeau, R. (2009). *Survey methodology* (2nd ed.). New York: Wiley.

Groves, R. M., & Tortora, R. D. (1991). Developing a system of indicators for unmeasured survey quality component. In: *Proceedings of the 48th Session of the ISI, Book 2, Cairo*.

Holmberg, A., Lorenc, B., & Werner, P. (2010). Contact strategies to improve participation via the web in a mixed-mode mail and web survey. *Journal of Official Statistics*, *26*(3), 465–480.

Hopkins, D., & King, G. (2010). Improving anchoring vignettes: Designing surveys to correct interpersonal incomparability. *Public Opinion Quarterly*, *74*, 201–222.

Israel, G. D. (2010). Effects of answer space size on responses to open-ended questions in mail surveys. *Journal of Official Statistics*, *26*(2), 271–285.

ITACOSM09: *First Italian Conference on Survey Methodology*. (2009). http://www.unisi.it/eventi/dmq2009/presentation.htm

Kateri, M., Kamps, U., & Balakrishnan, N. (2010). Multi-sample simple step-stress experiment under time constraints. *Statistica Neerlandica*, *64*(1), 77–96.

Kim, J. K., & Park, M. (2010). Calibration estimation in survey sampling. *International Statistical Review*, *78*(1), 21–39.

King, G., Murray, C., Salomon, J., & Tandon, A. (2004). Enhancing the validity and cross-cultural comparability of measurement in survey research. *American Political Science Review*, *98*, 191–205.

King, G., & Wand, J. (2007). Comparing incomparable survey responses: Evaluating and selecting anchoring vignettes. *Political Analysis*, *15*, 96–117.

Murphy, J., Eyerman, J., McCue, C., Hottinger, C., & Kennet, J. (2005). Interviewer falsification detection using data mining. In: *Proceedings of Statistics Canada Symposium 2005, Methodological Challenges for Future Information Needs, Canada*.

Pratesi, M., & Salvati, N. (2009). Small area estimation in the presence of correlated random area effects. *Journal of Official Statistics*, *25*(1), 37–53.

Razafindratsima, N., & Sarter, H. (2008). *Evaluation and treatment of non-response in the ELFE cohort: Results of the pilot studies*. Statistics Canada International Symposium, Canada.

SAE2007: *IASS Satellite Conference on Small Area Estimation*. (2007). http://www.dipstat.ec.unipi.it/SAE2007/

Särndal, C. E. (2007). The calibration approach in survey theory and practice. *Survey Methodology*, *33*, 99–119.

Schonlau, M., Van Soest, A., Kapteyn, A., Couper, M. P. (2006). *Selection bias in web surveys and the use of propensity scores*. Working Paper.

SS2010: *Workshop on "Statistical Surveys: thinking about methodology and applications"*. (2010). http://www.unimc.it/sviluppoeconomico/workshop-statistical-survey-thinking-about

Statistics Canada: Innovative methods for surveying difficult-to-reach populations. International Symposium (2004).

Tourangeau, R., Groves, R. M., Kennedy, C., & Yang, T. (2009). The presentation of a web survey, non-responses and measurement errors among member of web panel. *Journal of Official Statistics*, *25*(3), 299–321.

U.S. Bureau of Labor Statistics: *The B.L.S. quality measurement model*. (1994). Internal report, Washington, DC.

Van Tuinen, H. K. (2009). Research and development in official statistics and scientific co-operation with university: A follow-up study. *Journal of Official Statistics*, *25*(4), 467–482.

Verma, V., Gagliardi, F., & Ferretti, C. (2009). *On pooling of data and measures*. Working Paper No. 84, DMQ, University of Siena, Italy.

Werkhoven, T. (2004). *Improving the timeliness of short-term statistics*. CBS, Meeting of OECD Short-term Economic Statistics Expert Group, Chateau de la Muette, 28–30 June.

Yan, T., Curtin, R., & Jans, M. (2010). Trends in income nonresponse over two decades. *Journal of Official Statistics*, *26*(1), 145–164.

Zanutto, E., & Zaslavsky, A. (2002). Using administrative records to improve small area estimation: An example from U.S. decennial census. *Journal of Official Statistics*, *18*(4), 559–576.

Part II
Questionnaire Design

Measurement Scales for Scoring or Ranking Sets of Interrelated Items

Luigi Fabbris

Abstract Surveys concerned with human values, economic utilities, organisational features, customer or citizen satisfaction, or with preferences or choices among a set of items may aim at estimating either a ranking or a scoring of the choice set. In this paper we discuss the statistical and practical properties of five different techniques for data collection of a set of interrelated items; namely the ranking of items, the technique of picking the best/worst item, the partitioning of a fixed total among the items, the rating of each item and the paired comparison of all distinct pairs of items. Then, we discuss the feasibility of the use of each technique if a computer-assisted data-collection mode (e.g. CATI (telephone), CAPI (face-to-face), CAWI (web) or CASI (self-administered)) is adopted. The paper concludes with suggestions for the use of either technique in real survey contexts.

1 Introduction

In the following, we deal with survey procedures for the collection of data on a closed set of interrelated entities. The procedures apply to research situations in which questionnaires are administered to a population. The aim of these procedures is to elicit choices or preferences. For the sake of clarity, a choice applies to expressions such "*I choose that option*", while a preference applies to "*I prefer this instead of that*". In either case, a choice/preference criterion is to be specified.

In marketing studies, these procedures are called "stated preferences", as opposed to "revealed preferences" that stem from the observation of purchase data. The stated preference data aim at describing the world (market, society, community, etc.) as it could be; the revealed preference data represent the world as it is.

Luigi Fabbris (✉)
Statistics Department, University of Padua, Padua, Italy
e-mail: luigi.fabbris@unipd.it

C. Davino and L. Fabbris (eds.), *Survey Data Collection and Integration*,
DOI: 10.1007/978-3-642-21308-3_2, © Springer-Verlag Berlin Heidelberg 2013

It is assumed that the choice set is composed of p entities and that data are collected from n sample units. The data can be used to estimate either scores or ranks referred to as the choice set. Scores may be of interest to parameterise a function; for instance, to compose a complex indicator by combining a set of p elementary indicators for the final aim of partitioning resources among the units of a population. Ranks are appropriate, for instance, to define priorities among the choice set, to help communicators to make the public aware of hierarchies among the items, or to highlight the units that gained or lost positions with respect to a previous ranking.

As an example, if a budget is to be partitioned among the best-performing universities, quantitative and precise values are needed. If, instead, the best-performing universities are to be listed for guiding students who are choosing a university, the accuracy of the three top positions may suffice.

The data we are concerned with are normally administered as a battery of items under a common heading. The schemes of item presentation will be described in Sect. 2. We will also evaluate the procedures from the statistical (Sect. 3) and practical (Sect. 4) viewpoints with the aim of using either procedure in a computer-assisted survey. In Sect. 5, some general conclusions will be presented.

2 Survey Procedures

To collect choice or preference data, a battery of questions is to be administered to a sample of n ($n \geq 1$) individuals. Let us suppose that the choice set is selected from the universe of all possible sets that satisfy certain statistical properties. The following techniques will be examined: ranking (Sect. 2.1), picking the best/worst item (Sect. 2.2), partitioning a fixed budget (Sect. 2.3), rating (Sect. 2.4) and comparing in pairs (Sect. 2.5). An example of how a choice set can be constructed for a conjoint analysis[1] will be presented, as well (Sect. 2.6).

2.1 Ranking

The final result of the application of a ranking technique to a sample of respondents is a sequence from the most relevant item to last, according to an underlying construct. The procedure requires that each respondent evaluate all the items of the set simultaneously. Figure 1 is a scheme of a typical question for ranking purposes.

The technique may be administered in other formats whose common purpose is to determine a hierarchy of the p items, normally without ties. Ties may be allowed if the researcher perceives that the task required is too difficult for respondents. An alternative procedure that generates a ranking is the request of a sequence of choices

---

[1] Conjoint analysis is a multivariate method of statistical analysis of a set of alternatives each of which is qualified by two or more joint categories.

Heading: *"Please, carefully read the following list of items and indicate your order of importance in the side boxes from the most (1) to the least (p) important for (criterion)"*
Item list in random order, each item a row   **Box: Preference order**

Fig. 1 Scheme of a question for ranking a choice set

Heading: *"Please, carefully read the following list of items and indicate which one you consider the most/least important for (criterion) in the box underneath"*
Item list in random order, each item a row   **Box: Most/least important item**

Fig. 2 Scheme of a question on picking the best/worst item

of the kind "best-worst": initially, the choice of the best and worst items is performed using all p-listed alternatives, the second using the $p - 2$ remaining alternatives, and so on with two divergent choices at a time until the list exhausts. Munson and McIntyre (1979) and McCarty and Shrum (1997, 2000) call this stepwise ranking *"sequential most-least procedure"*.

2.2 Picking the Best/Worst Item

If ranking is not possible in full, each respondent may be asked to pick the most valued item and in case the least valued item on the list. Other names for this technique include *most/least* and *max difference analysis*. Figure 2 is a scheme of a typical question for obtaining this objective.

Respondents are sometimes asked to pick k ($k < p$) items as the most/least preferable ones and, in some instances, to select the best/worst item among the k. In other cases, the request could be just to select the k most/least preferable items out of the choice set. This more complex procedure will be named *"pick k out of p items"*. Even the method of picking one or more items requires the simultaneous contrast of the whole set of entities, but the procedure is much less demanding for respondents than full ranking because just a few items are pre-selected for top or bottom positions after a first reading of the list.

2.3 Fixed Total Partitioning

A respondent is assigned a fixed budget of, let's say, 100 points, and is asked to partition it over the p items according to some criterion. This procedure is also named *"budget partitioning"*. Figure 3 is a scheme of a question for fixed total partitioning.

If a computer-assisted interviewing system is applied, it is possible to check the sum of points spent after each assignment. Conrad et al. (2005) found that running

> **Heading**: *"Please, consider a budget of 100 points to be partitioned among the following items. Indicate in the side boxes how many points you would assign to each item according to (importance criterion)"*
> **Item list in random order, each item a row**   **Box: Assigned points**

Fig. 3 Scheme of a question for fixed total partitioning

> **Heading**: *"Please, assign an importance score between 1 and c, where 1 is the minimum and c the maximum, to each of the following items"*
> **Item list in random order, each item a row**   *Minimum=*① ② ③ ..... ©*=Maximum*

Fig. 4 Scheme of a question on rating individual items

totals improved the likelihood that the final tally matched the given sum, led to more edits of the individual items (the Authors considered this occurrence a symptom of the importance attributed by respondents to the required task) and took the respondents less time. A researcher can decide whether to insist that the respondent adjusts the assigned points if their sum does not fit the fixed total. Each item i $(i = 1, \ldots, p)$ is assigned by a respondent a "quantum" of a criterion, e.g. importance, relatively to the overall budget. It is relevant for survey purposes that respondents can assign no points at all to unimportant items, a possibility that is excluded if the rating technique is applied.

Any point assignment is an interval score that can be contrasted with the scores of the other $(p - 1)$ items and the scores given by other respondents to item i. A researcher who does not rely on the obtained values may retain just the ordinal hierarchies between the items, transforming in this way the data into a ranking.

2.4 Rating Individual Items

The respondent is asked to assign each item i $(i = 1, \ldots, p)$ an independent value according to either an ordinal (Likert-type) or an interval scale. The measurement scale is the same for all items. In general, in each row, there is the item description and a common scale with the so-called anchor points (minimum and maximum) at the extremes (see Fig. 4). With reference to weights estimation, the technique is sometime called "absolute measurement".

A possible improvement to the simple rating technique is the combination of two methods; for instance, that of picking the most and the least important items and then rating all the items in the usual way (Krosnick and Alwin 1988) or to rank-and-rate as suggested by McCarty and Shrum (2000).

> **Heading**: *"Please, choose an item out of each pair we will submit to you in sequence. Which item is more important to you with reference to (criterion) between (1) and (2)?"... "And between (1) and (3)?"......*
> **List of pairs in a convenient order**   **Box: Item chosen within the pair**

Fig. 5 Scheme of the administration of $p(p-1)/2$ paired comparisons

2.5 Paired Comparisons

Each respondent is administered all the $p(p-1)/2$ pairs of items and asked to choose the preferable item of any pair according to a predefined criterion. Ties may be admitted to avoid forcing reluctant respondents. Figure 5 is a scheme of question for paired comparisons.

Saaty (1977) proposes a variant of the full pair comparison technique. His technique involves submitting to a single volunteer ($n = 1$) the whole set of the $p(p-1)/2$ pairs asking him or her not only which is the best item for each pair (i, j) but also how many times item i is more preferable than item j.

In addition, Clemans (1966) proposes a paired comparison system that is more complex than the basic one. It involves assigning a respondent 3 points for every two items of a pair so that the possible outcomes are $(3,0)$, $(2,1)$, $(1,2)$, $(0,3)$, yielding for each comparison a more differentiated outcome than the simple choice between the paired items.

If p is large, any paired comparison system is not viable even if visual aids and interviewers are invested. For this reason a reduced form of preference elicitation may be adopted that limits response burden. One of these techniques is the *tournament* technique as proposed by Fabbris and Fabris (2003). This involves (i) ordering the set of p items according to a criterion and (ii) submitting for choice in a hierarchical fashion the $p/2$ pairs of adjacent items, then the $p/4$ pairs of items preferred at the first level of choice, and so on until the most preferred item is sorted out. The choice may be structured by composing pairs or triplets of items at all levels (for more details see Sect. 4.5).

2.6 Conjoint Attribute Measurement

All the procedures presented in the previous sections apply for a conjoint analysis of sets of attributes. Conjoint measurement requires the definition of a set of alternatives that respondents have to rank, pick the best, rate or compare in pairs. Each alternative is specified as a set of attributes belonging to variables common to all alternatives. For instance, a conjoint measurement for market research purposes may be set up as in Fig. 6.

The four alternatives, also called "prop cards" (Green et al. 2001), are the logical product of two variables with two categories each and a related price/cost. Imagine,

Alternative A	Alternative B	Alternative C	Alternative D
$V_1=1$	$V_1=1$	$V_1=2$	$V_1=2$
$V_2=1$	$V_2=2$	$V_2=1$	$V_2=2$
Price: level 1	Price: level 2	Price: level 3	Price: level 4

Fig. 6 Example of items for a conjoint measurement

for instance, the transportation alternatives for reaching the university campus from a nearby town: the V_is denote variables that might influence the students' choice (e.g. travel time, schedule, comfort and so on), and $V_i = j$ means that option j of variable V_i is specified.

The alternatives are presented in a simplified way, often illustrated by a photo or other visual representation that helps respondents to associate each alternative to its price, consciously contrasting the offered alternatives and evaluating the trade-offs between alternatives (Gustafsson et al. 2007). Conjoint analysis assumes that alternatives compensate each other, meaning that a trade-off exists between alternatives. This may be inadequate in the case of immoral or dangerous alternatives; for instance, an alternative may be a fatal level of pollution. Hence, the researcher should ignore alternatives that may be dangerous over a certain threshold.

Conjoint measurement can compare several alternatives. Even if the alternatives are qualified by variables whose number of categories to be crossed is large, the presentation can be simplified by planning an experiment that drastically reduces the number of cross-categories. Readers interested in this type of experiments could consult, among others, Green and Srinivasan (1990), Elrod et al. (1993), Kuhfeld et al. (1994) and Louvriere et al. (2000).

3 Statistical Properties of the Scales

Let us consider the aim of estimating the population values of the p items on the basis of the preferences x_{hi} expressed by individual h ($h = 1, \ldots, n$) for item i ($i = 1, \ldots, p$). A function $g(X_i)$ links the possible responses to the latent value ξ_i of item i:

$$g(X_i) = \xi_i + \varepsilon_i \quad i = (1, \ldots, p), \tag{1}$$

where ε_i is an error term that accounts for the sampling error, c_i, and the observational error, r_i, inherent to item i:

$$\varepsilon_i = c_i + r_i \quad i = (1, \ldots, p). \tag{2}$$

Sampling and response errors are independent of each other and can be evaluated separately. The sampling error depends on the sampling design, and its evaluation is beyond the scope of this paper.[2] The response error is composed of systematic ("bias") and random components. The systematic component is common to all respondents, is constant regardless of the number of obtained responses and is at risk of being confused with the latent value ξ_i. The random errors vary within and between individuals. Response errors vary according to the following:

- *The respondent's answering style*, e.g. his or her capacity and willingness to respond correctly (Baumgartner and Steenkamp 2001). The individual error may be either random (zero mean in repeated surveys) or systematic (constant over repeated surveys).
- *Group response biases*, i.e. common to a population segment or common to the whole assignment of an interviewer or supervisor. They are measurable as within-group correlated response errors (Harzing et al. 2009).
- *The survey context*, i.e. the set of social and physical characteristics of the interview setting. A non-neutral setting may generate systematic errors (Swait and Adamowicz 1996).

The expected value of the random error is nil across repeated measurements, but if the response error is correlated within groups of respondents, it may have a negative impact on the response variance of estimates (Fellegi 1964; Bassi and Fabbris 1997). Group response biases and interviewer biases belong to the family of intra-class correlated errors.[3]

The latent value ξ_i is the population value of item i that represents an aspect of the concept underlying all the items of a set. Values may relate to human life principles (Rokeach 1967, 1979); consumers or citizens' preferences (Beatty et al. 1985); economic utility of facts, goods or services (Small and Rosen 1981); criteria for organizational decisions (Crosby et al. 1990; Aloysius et al. 2006) and so on. In econometric theory, ξ_i is the utility associated with the ith alternative; in consumer preference theory it is the individual part-worth parameter of an aspect related to a common construct; in multi-criteria decision support systems, it represents the acceptability of a decision after a holistic assessment of the alternatives.

Some scholars handle the response errors that may have crept into the data by specifying the functional structure of the variance of the unobserved effects. For instance, Swait and Adamowicz (1996) hypothesise that the variance associated with an element of the choice set is a function of the task complexity. Others (Bhat 1997; Hensher 1998) use respondents' characteristics as proxies for the ability to comprehend the variability of response tasks. All choice data allow the estimation of both aggregative and individual models. The latter estimates can be aggregated at a second stage of analysis to obtain cluster estimates.

If the data are observed on an interval scale and ordered in an $(n \times p)$ matrix $\mathbf{X} = \{x_{hi}(h = 1, \ldots, n; i = 1, \ldots, p)\}$ with columns that sum to zero over the n obtained responses $[E(\mathbf{X}) = \mathbf{0}]$, the variance-covariance matrix $\mathbf{S}$ of the items is:

---

[2] Readers may refer to Kish (1965) for a comprehensive manual.

[3] The family of intra-class correlated errors also includes measures of the so-called "normative" scores (Cattell 1944), which are the scores of an individual that depend upon the scores of other individuals in the population.

$$S = X^T X/n \tag{3}$$

where X^T denotes the transpose of X. If item variances equal 1, a correlation matrix R is obtained. Both S and R matrices are square $(n \times n)$, symmetric $(s_{ij} = s_{ji}; r_{ij} = r_{ji}, i \neq j = 1, \ldots, p)$ and positive semidefinite, that is $\rho(X) = \rho(S) = \rho(R)$, where ρ $(\rho \leq p)$ denotes the matrix rank. Ideally, an X matrix, or a convenient transformation of it, is one-dimensional, so that the underlying preferences can be located along the real axis represented by the first unique factor.

The one-dimensionality of matrix R should be tested before the estimation of the latent values. An advance processing of the data via a principal component analysis may be used to explain the items' variance. In general, about 70 % of the observed variance should be explained by the first principal component. If the pattern exhibits more than one dimension, it may be appropriate to restrain the choice set. If an advance testing is not possible, theory on the subject matter can help the researcher in selecting the items.

If the data are observed with a scale that is at least ordinal, a preference, or dominance, matrix P can be computed whose diagonal elements are null and whose off diagonal cells contain measures of preference/dominance. The generic element p_{ij} $(i \neq j = 1, \ldots, p)$ of P is a measure of the dominance of the row item i over the column item j.

The properties of P depend on the data-collection technique. If p_{ij} assumes values constrained between 0 and 1, the symmetric element is its complement to one $(p_{ji} = 1 - p_{ij})$. If $p_{ij} = 0.5$, no preference can be expressed between i and j. If p_{ij} is larger than 0.5, it means that $i > j$ (i dominates j), and the closer the value to 1, the larger the dominance. Of course, if p_{ij} is lower than 0.5, the opposite is true; that is, $i < j$. The P matrix is anti-symmetric $(p_{ji} = 1 - p_{ij})$ and of full rank $[\rho(P) = p]$. The estimates of ξ_i rely on the Euclidean distances between preferences (Brunk 1960; Brauer and Gentry 1968).

If Saaty's (1977) approach is adopted, the generic element of $P = \{p_{ij}, i \neq j = 1, \ldots, p\}$ may assume any positive value. The Author suggests that p_{ij} values vary between $1/k$ and k, where k is the maximum level of dominance of i over j; for instance, if $k = 9$ and $p_{ij} = 9$ it means that i is nine times more preferable than j. The equilibrium value between i and j is $p_{ij} = 1$. The value in position (j, i), symmetric to (i, j), is its inverse $(p_{ji} = 1/p_{ij})$. The estimates of ξ_i rely on the ratio structure of P.

It is possible to construct a matrix P with any data-collection technique presented in Sect. 2. The ordinal relationship between any two items may be transformed into a dominance relationship $(i > j)$:

$$y_{hij} = 1 \quad \text{if } x_{hi} > x_{hj} \quad (h = 1, \ldots, n; i \neq j = 1, \ldots, p) \tag{4}$$

and 0 otherwise. A tie $(x_{hi} = x_{hj})$ implies no dominance relationship between i and j. For instance, if a pick-the-best technique were applied, the transformation of a choice into a 0/1 value would be based on the dominance relationships between the best item (1) and all other items (i.e. $y_{h(1)j} = 1$ for all js) or the dominance between the worst item (p) and the intermediate ones (i.e. $y_{hj(p)} = 1$ for all js).

If a fixed-budget procedure were adopted and the researcher did not rely on the interval property of the data, the individual data would be considered ranks, and the conversion formula 4 could be applied. Besides, ratings can be downgraded to ranks by merely considering the dominance relations between any two items i and j.

We can estimate a vector of ξ_i values if $\mathbf{P}$ is irreducible; that is, if all values of $\mathbf{P}$ except those on the main diagonal are positive. According to the Perron-Frobenius theorem (Brauer 1957; Brauer and Gentry 1968), the right eigenvector $\mathbf{w}$ associated with the largest positive eigenvalue, λ_{max}, of matrix $\mathbf{P}$ is obtained as:

$$\mathbf{P}\mathbf{w} = \lambda_{max}\mathbf{w} \quad \left(\mathbf{w}^T\mathbf{w} = 1\right). \tag{5}$$

The elements of $\mathbf{w} = \{w_i, i = 1, \ldots, p\}$ are proportional to those of the vector of estimates $\xi' = \{\xi_i, i = 1, \ldots, p\}$. If the ξ_is add up to one ($\sum_i \xi_i = 1$), it is possible to estimate a latent value as (Fabbris 2010):

$$\hat{\xi}_i = w_i \bigg/ \sum_i w_i \quad (i = 1, \ldots, p). \tag{6}$$

If the sample of respondents shows a consistent pattern, then all rows of the preference matrix are linearly dependent. Thus, the latent preferences are consistently estimated by values of a single row of the matrix but a multiplicative constant. All data-collection techniques introduced in Sect. 1 give about the same results in terms of relative importance of the choice set (Alwin and Krosnick 1985; Kamakura and Mazzon 1991). A way to discriminate between techniques is by analysing the reliability and validity of the obtainable responses. A data-collection technique is *reliable* if it produces accurate data in any circumstance. Reliability can be assessed through multiple measurements of the phenomenon and evaluation of the consistency of measures. A battery of items is *valid* if the obtainable data represent the phenomenon the researcher had in mind. The validity refers to the items and scales' construction techniques apt to represent the content domain. In the following, our considerations will be referred not to the single answers but to the overall correlation pattern and to the preference of each item over the others.

3.1 Ranking

The relationship between the items' rankings and the underlying values is:

$$P\left(x_i \geq x_j\right) = P\left(\xi_i \geq \xi_j\right) \quad (i \neq j = 1, \ldots, p) \tag{7}$$

where $P(a)$ denotes the probability of the argument a. The error terms ε_i and ε_j $(i \neq j = 1, \ldots, p)$ correlate with each other because of the fixed total, T, of the ranks elicited from any individual $[T = p(p + 1)/2]$. This condition—called "ipsative" (from the Latin *ipse*; see Cattell 1944; Clemans 1966) or "compensative", since a large assignment to an item is at the expense of the other items—causes the error terms to be unduly negatively correlated both within an individual (Chan and Bentler 1993) and through the whole sample (Vanleeuwen and Mandabach 2002). The ipsative condition induces into the correlation matrix $\mathbf{R}$ several undue negative correlations. These negative correlations depend on the data-collection technique and not on the effective values, ξ_is, of the items. The factor configuration of ipsative measures may differ from the proper underlying configuration. Clemans (1966) showed that not only the factors of an ipsatised matrix $\mathbf{R}^*$

$$\mathbf{R}^* = \mathbf{D}^{-1/2}\mathbf{S}^*\mathbf{D}^{-1/2},$$
$$\mathbf{D} = diag\left\{s_{ii}^* \ (i = 1, \ldots, p)\right\},$$
$$\mathbf{S}^* = \left(\mathbf{I} - \mathbf{11}^T/p\right)\mathbf{S}\left(\mathbf{I} - \mathbf{11}^T/p\right),$$

where $\mathbf{S}$ is the observed variance-covariance matrix, may differ from those of the raw data matrix $\mathbf{R}$ because of the large number of negative correlations, but also the rank of $\mathbf{R}^*$ is one less than that of $\mathbf{R}$. Moreover, a factor accounting for the methodological choices may stem from factor analysis. This factor, which could come out after two or three proper factors, is to be removed from the analysis of factors. Besides, the factor analysis of rankings highlights a number of factors lower than the number obtainable with ratings. Munson and McIntyre (1979) found that the correlations implied by the latter technique require about three times as many factors as the former technique.

A least-square solution for predicting a criterion variable with ipsative data is identical to the least-square solution where one variable of the ipsative set is removed before the regression analysis. The removal of a variable is a trick for coefficient estimation because of the singularity of ipsatised matrix $\mathbf{X}^*$. The proportion of deviance explained by the ipsatised data is measured by the squared multiple correlation coefficient,

$$R^{*2} = R^2 - \left(\sum_i^p \beta_i\right)^2 \bigg/ \sum_{ij}^p \rho_{ij}^-, \tag{8}$$

where ρ_{ij}^- is the generic element of $\mathbf{R}^{-1}$, and $R^{*2} \leq R^2$. The operational difficulties caused by ipsatised data make it clear that a researcher should strive to obtain absolute, instead of ipsative or ipsatised measures.

The larger the number of items to be ranked, the less reliable are the obtainable rankings. It is easy to guess that the rankings' reliability is high for the most liked and disliked items and lower for those in the middle. It is not possible, however, to evaluate the reliability and validity of the ranks of the items that would never be chosen in any foreseeable circumstances and of those that are obscure or meaningless to respondents.

A good property of the ranking technique is that the measurement scale does not need to be anchored at the extremes. This favours this technique if the extremes are undefined; for instance, if the extremes are to be translated in a multilingual research study. If an individual's ranking is fully expressed, a "strong order" of the items is evident that may be used for either scoring or ranking the items (Coombs 1976). The ipsative property is irrelevant for the estimation of ξ_is if they are estimated via a preference analysis.[4]

3.2 Pick the Best/Worst

The relationship between the items' choices and the underlying values is:

$$P\left(x_{(1)} \geq x_{(i)}\right) = P\left(\xi_{(1)} \geq \xi_{(i)}\right) \quad (i \neq (1), \ldots, p) \tag{9}$$

where $x_{(1)}$ denotes the item selected as best. An analogous formula applies for $x_{(p)}$, the worst item. This procedure generates data that are "weakly ordered", since a complete ordering cannot be determined for the items (Louvriere et al. 2000). Nevertheless, a preference matrix $\mathbf{P}$ can be estimated if a sufficiently large number of individuals are surveyed on a common choice set.

If the ξ_is are non-compensatory,[5] the pick-the-best strategy is preferable in spite of its simplicity. In all bounded-rationality contexts and, in particular, in social and psychological studies, this strategy showed particular plausibility (Martignon and Hoffrage 2002).

3.3 Fixed Budget Partitioning

The relationship between the preferences expressed for the items and their underlying values is:

$$E\left(x_i\right) = \xi_i + \varepsilon_i \quad (i = 1, \ldots, p) \tag{10}$$

where $E\left(\varepsilon_i\right) = 0$ and $E\left(\varepsilon_i \varepsilon_j\right) \neq 0$. Since this technique is fixed total (i.e. ipsative), the response errors correlate with each other, in the negative direction. The maximum likelihood expectation of x_i is the arithmetic mean of the observed values over the

---

[4] Even if an ipsative data-collection technique forces undue correlations on response errors, it may be worthwhile to "ipsatise" a data matrix $\mathbf{X}$ if the researcher is interested in the analysis of the differences between rows (i.e. between single individual's scores). A matrix may be ipsatised by adding a suitable constant to the scores of a respondent (i.e. to the scores of a row) so that all the new column scores sum to the same constant (Cunningham et al. 1977). Columns of matrix $\mathbf{X}$ may be rescaled to zero-mean and unit-variance, either before or after ipsatisation.

[5] Suppose the ξ_is are ordered from smallest to largest; they are non-compensatory if each ξ_i ($i > j = 1, \ldots, p - 1$) is larger than the sum of all ξ_is that are smaller than it (i.e.: $\xi_j > \sum_{i > j} \xi_i$).

respondents, irrespective of eventual ties. Although quantitative, the data collected with this technique ignore the absolute relevance of the evaluated items for a respondent. Let us consider, for instance, two respondents, A and B, whose effective levels of importance over four items are the following:

A: Family = 90, Work = 80, Hobbies = 70, Religion = 60;
B: Family = 70, Work = 60, Hobbies = 50, Religion = 40.

It is evident that A places systematically larger importance on any specific item than B. However, these differences do not transpire from the data collection if an ipsative data-collection technique is adopted. In fact, the following considerations apply:

- Their rankings are the same, the orders being independent of the intensity of the underlying construct.
- Since the distances between the items are the same, if budget constraints are introduced, the item distribution is the same for the two individuals.
- A and B differentiate the items in the same way, unless a ratio-based technique is taken instead of a difference-based one.[6] Even the item variances and the inter-item covariance are the same for the two individuals.

3.4 Rating

The relationship between an item score and its underlying value is:

$$E(x_i) = \xi_i + \varepsilon_i \quad (i = 1, \ldots, p) \tag{11}$$

where $E(\varepsilon_i) = 0$. The maximum likelihood expectation of x_i is the average of the observed values over all respondents. The hypothesis of a null correlation between error terms ($E(\varepsilon_i \varepsilon_j) = 0$) holds if the individual's responses given on previous items have no necessary effect on the following ones. This is sometimes called "procedural independence" (Louvriere et al. 2000). The hypothesis of procedural independence does not hold if the order of administration affects the responses given after the first one. It may be argued, in fact, that the respondent focuses the underlying concept along the sequence of his or her given responses so that the preferences expressed from the second item on are anchored to the preference assigned to the previous items. In this case, the validity of responses improves from the first to the last response, but the reliability of responses diminishes because response errors correlate with each other.

One of the main drawbacks of the rating technique is the non-differentiation of responses. This means that respondents tend to dump responses towards an extreme

---

[6] It may be hypothesised that responses possess the ratio property, which means that the ratio between two values is logically justified. The ipsative constraint implies, instead, that only the interval scale properties apply to fixed-total data.

of the scale, usually its maximum, making it difficult the discrimination between item scores (Alwin and Krosnick 1985; Krosnick and Alwin 1988; McCarty and Shrum 1997; Jacoby 2011). Other respondents can use just a few points of the offered scale, and this makes the scores dependent on respondents' styles (Harzing et al. 2009).

The peculiarity of the use of scale points by a respondent can be measured with the variance between the category-values he or she uses to rate the items, that is:

$$V_h = \sum_i^p (x_{hi} - \bar{x}_h)^2 / p \quad (h = 1, \ldots, n), \tag{12}$$

where $\bar{x}_h = \sum_i^p x_{hi}/p$. This variance can be standardised with its maximum in the hypothesis that each item is assigned a different score and $p < k$, where k is the number of category-values of the scale:

$$\tilde{V}_h = V_h / \max (V_h) = 12 V_h / \left(k^2 - 1\right). \tag{13}$$

The standardised score, $\tilde{V}_h$, varies between zero and one and is close to zero if just a few category-values are used by individual h to rate the choice set. The lower this variance the more the scale is prone to response style.[7] This type of individual clustering of responses induces a positive correlation among the stated preferences. A combined method of picking the best and/or the worst items and then rating all the p items, as suggested by Krosnick and Alwin (1988), may be a solution for non-differentiation. The non-differentiation problem may be due to the low concentration of respondents while they answer the questionnaires; hence, the more demanding the questions, the larger the likelihood they will concentrate before answering. Nevertheless, several authors state that rating is superior in validity, certainly in comparison with ranking (Rankin and Grube 1980; Maio et al. 1996).

3.5 Paired Comparisons

The relationship between the frequency with which item i is preferred to item j and its underlying value, in an additive data-collection model, is the following:

$$p_{ij} = \xi_i - \xi_j + \varepsilon_{ij} \quad (i \neq j = 1, \ldots, p), \tag{14}$$

where p_{ij} is the observed frequency of the choices expressed by all sample units to whom the pair (i, j) was administered:

---

[7] Krosnick and Alwin (1988) propose Gini's measure if the researcher assumes a non-interval scale $V_h = 1 - \sum_j^k p_{hj}^2$ where p_{hj} is the frequency of point j in a scale of k points.

$$p_{ij} = \sum_{h}^{n} y_{hij}/n_{ij} \quad (i \neq j = 1, \ldots, p), \tag{15}$$

and ε_{ij} is the error term associated with the (i, j) comparison. Basically, the response error depends on the order of administration of the pair. The response error increases with the number of questions because of the respondent's fatigue; on the contrary, as the pair administration proceeds, the respondent focuses the content more and more clearly, and his or her responses become more conscious. An order effect on responses is unavoidable regardless of the sequence of administered pairs (Brunk 1960; Chrzan 1994; *contra*: Scheffé 1952). This effect is practically impossible to detect in a single-shot survey unless the administration order is randomised. Randomisation is possible if the survey is computer-assisted. If the administration of pairs is random, the order effect on responses vanishes on the average over the sample of respondents.

A desired property of the expressed preferences is that respondents' choices be transitive across the full set of choices (Coombs 1976). This property is based on the consistency requirement between all preferences that involve the ith item for the estimation of ξ_i values. The transition rule considers the paired relations of preferences between any three items, i, j and k. It can be said that $i > j$ if $i > k$ and $k > j$, where k is any item of the choice set but i and j. In terms of matrix $\mathbf{P}$ elements:

$$p_{ij} \geq p_{ik} \quad \text{if } p_{ik} \geq p_{kj} \geq 0.5 \quad (k \neq i \neq j = 1, \ldots, p), \tag{16}$$

$$p_{ij} \leq p_{ik} \quad \text{if } p_{ik} \leq p_{kj} \leq 0.5 \quad (k \neq i \neq j = 1, \ldots, p). \tag{17}$$

The application of transition rules makes the tournament technique viable. The application of a transition rule to estimate a preference between two missing pairs implies the computation of the estimates of p_{ij} through all possible ks and the synthesis (usually the average) of the estimated preferences. Transition rules may also be used to evaluate the internal consistency of a $\mathbf{P}$ matrix. It is possible, in fact, that any three preferences p_{ij}, p_{ik} and p_{kj} are not mutually coherent. Any inconsistency among such a triad may be considered a symptom either of a measurement error or of (logical) inner incoherence. The inconsistency of a set of preferences can be hypothesised as proportional to the number of triads that do not satisfy the rank-order preservation rule. Fabbris (2011) proposes an index of inconsistency based on the ratio between the number of incoherent triads and its maximum value under the full inconsistency hypothesis.

4 Practical Considerations

The feasibility of the preference elicitation techniques will be examined from the following viewpoints:

- *Respondent burden*; that is, time and physical and psychological effort required from responding individuals.
- *Expected proportion* of missing values. It is a measure of the items' expected difficulty or of negative attitudes toward the survey content among the interviewees. The higher the proportion of missing values, the higher the risk that the collected data ignore specific segments of the surveyed population.
- *Possibility of application* with a face-to-face (CAPI) or telephone (CATI) interviewing system, or any kind of online procedure (e.g. through the web, email or other online procedures (CAWI), self-administered (CASI) or mail questionnaire).

The same order of presentation of the preference elicitation techniques as Sect. 2 will be followed.

4.1 Ranking

The difficulty of the respondent task increases substantially with p, the number of items. In fact, it can be guessed that a typical respondent reads and compares all the items to identify the most and/or the least important items. Then, a series of multiple comparisons is required for respondents to define the second best and the following positions. The "best-worst" procedure introduced in Sect. 2.1 may be a rationalisation of the foregoing dynamics. Even if it is generally unknown how the respondent performs his or her task, the best-worst sequence can reduce respondent acquiescence (McCarty and Shrum 1997).

What makes the ranking technique generally acceptable is that respondents are accustomed to ranking provided ties are allowed and the number of items is reasonable. Several scholars (including Rokeach and Ball Rokeach 1989, among others), balancing the likely response burden with the wealth of information contained in a ranking, and assuming that this technique forces participants to differentiate between similarly regarded techniques, propose ranking as the preferable technique regardless of the self-administered survey mode (CAWI, CASI, mail).

Ranking is not feasible in a CATI survey, because it is necessary for the respondent to examine repeatedly the set of alternatives, and this is feasible only if the respondent can memorise the item list. Whatever the device applied to exhibit the item list, the results differ according to respondent personality; also, embarrassing pauses and unwanted hints from the interviewer may condition the respondent's task. Even in a face-to-face survey, the presence of an interviewer may bother or embarrass the respondent during such a task. This difficulty may be attenuated if interviewers are specifically trained.

If respondents are insufficiently motivated to collaborate, the extreme choices (e.g. the top and bottom items) may be accurately elicited, but the intermediate positions may be uncertain. That is why under a difficult survey conditions (for instance, if the data are collected in a hurry or the interviewee is standing), the simple pick-the-best/worst technique is advisable. Another difficult task may be that of collecting data on non-choices (e.g. the ordering of a set of alternatives the respondent would never choose). Louvriere et al. (2000) suggest not considering ranking as an appropriate procedure in this regard.

4.2 Picking the Best/Worst

This procedure is the least-burdening among those that require respondents to evaluate a whole set of alternatives at a time, for just the extremes are to be chosen. It may be considered a truncated form of the complex tasks required by the ranking technique. It can be applied easily with any interviewer-based (CAPI) or self-administered (CASI, CAWI, mail) questionnaire. It can be applied in a CATI survey only if the list to be remembered is short.

4.3 Fixed Total Partitioning

The fixed total technique is burdensome and time consuming for respondents, because it requires not only the ranking of the item set but also the quantitative valuing of each item. If the choice set is large, it is possible to break it into categories and then ask respondents to prioritise the items within each category.

The responses obtained with the fixed total procedure are subject to response style, since it remains unknown how a respondent performs the required multiple task; namely, ranking the alternatives, assigning them a value, checking the score total and adjusting the scores according to the given budget. As an example, it may happen that a mathematically minded respondent starts his or her task by dividing the budget by the number of items to have a first idea of the average score and then picks the top item and possibly the second best or the bottom item with a mechanism similar to that of the picking-the-best technique. Then, he or she has to rate them, maybe by choosing a differentiation-from-average criterion. It is clear that the task is highly burdensome, more than any ranking or rating procedure, and that the intermediate scores are precarious.

Hence, this technique is prohibitive in CATI surveys for the same reasons put forward for ranking. It is plausible that respondents collaborate in full if an interviewer is present where the respondents gather (CAPI mode) and are motivated to collaborate in the survey.

It is an acceptable procedure for self-administered surveys provided the respondent population is sympathetic to the research aims and the questionnaire is communicative. In self-administered surveys, in fact, the respondents try to seek information from the instrument itself (Ganassali 2008).

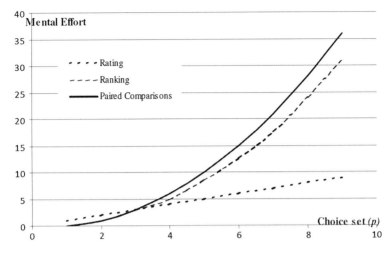

Fig. 7 Respondents' mental effort hypothesised in performing ranking, rating and paired comparison procedures

4.4 Rating

Rating single items is the easiest procedure among those presented in Sect. 2, since people are asked to assign a value to each alternative and the time and fatigue associated with their task is about linear (i.e. proportional to the number of items). The superiority of the rating versus the ranking procedure from the viability viewpoint becomes larger and larger as the number of items diverges. In Fig. 7, the lower straight line represents the expected respondent fatigue if the rating procedure is applied, and the dotted curve represents[8] that of ranking.

The two techniques diverge notably as burden is concerned for p larger than three or four. The curve representing the burden of the fixed-total procedure might be even steeper than ranking. However, ratings are prone both to social desirability biases and to difficult discrimination between items. For instance, suppose that customer preferences for innovations in urban bus transportation are to be elicited and juxtapose the alternative of modifying the bus structure to favour the boarding of the disabled and that of increasing the night services for all customers. It is reasonable to expect high scores for both items (devices for the disabled and night services) if rating is applied; however, night services might get much higher preferences if either ranking or pair comparison is applied. In fact, a respondent's choice that refers to his or her

---

[8] The curve representing the effort due to ranking was traced by assuming that reading, memorising and ordering an item with respect to the previous item (ranking task) implies to a respondent the same fatigue as reading and assigning a score to an item (rating task). The ideal respondent should repeat the set of memorisation and ordering for all items but those already ranked. The burden guessed for the ranking task is probably an underestimate of the fatigue a conscious respondent would put in performing his or her task. Munson and McIntyre (1979) state that ranking takes about three times longer than comparable rating.

Fig. 8 Hierarchical tournament structure, $p = 8$

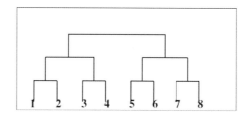

own utility tends to discriminate among the possible items, while the independent evaluation of a single item may be conditioned by social desirability. Moshkovich et al. (1998) even found that if items are important to respondents, they tend to rate them lower than if items are insignificant to them, since they hypothesize that people tend to score highly if the subject matter is socially marginal.

4.5 Paired Comparisons

The choice of the preferred alternative when items are administered in pairs is very burdensome. It requires a lot of respondents' time and causes mental fatigue, because a choice is to be made for all distinct pairs. The difficulty associated with the respondent's task is larger if the paired items logically overlap or if their marginal rate of substitution is high (Bettman et al. 1993). This implies that this procedure cannot be applied in full if p is larger than four, unless respondents are faithful. In Fig. 7, it is hypothesized that paired comparison is more burdensome than ranking.

If p is large, it is possible to classify the items in homogeneous categories and perform first the paired comparisons within each category and then compare the categories. This makes the direct comparison between the unmatched items impossible.

Another reduced version of paired comparisons, such as the tournament technique or an incomplete experimental design, is usually necessary regardless of the survey mode. Figure 8 represents an administration scheme of the latter technique with $p = 8$. More complex structures can be applied for a number p of items that is a multiple of either two or three (Fabbris and Fabris 2003). The tournament technique requires the administration of just $(p - 1)$ questions, instead of $p(p - 1)/2$, and is acceptable if the initial coupling of items is randomised. The tournament technique may be set up for any kind of computer assisted interviewing if an expert is available for computer programming. Programming assistance is required, in particular, because the randomisation of pairs implies the necessity of typing the unordered responses within appropriate fields in the database. The random presentation of pairs to the respondent is also a solution for eliminating the order effect if the complete paired comparison procedure is adopted. Hence, a computer-assisted data-collection system is particularly appropriate regardless of the choice-based technique, administered either with the mediation of an interviewer or without it. The paired comparison technique is not viable in remote surveys (CATI, CAWI, mail).

5 Concluding remarks

The most diffused techniques for collecting data on sets of interrelated items have been examined. The analysis was held with reference to both statistical and practical paradigms. No technique showed enough positive properties to make it preferable in all survey situations. The feasibility of the scales was based chiefly on the burden posed on respondents to perform their task. The respondent burden correlates with the quantity, reliability and validity of the information expected from responses; in particular, the more demanding the task, the lower the sample coverage and the higher the frequency and variety of errors. Therefore, the researcher should make his or her methodological choices balancing the tolerable burden and the expected information according to the population at hand.

Choosing the appropriate scale requires an analysis of the research context at the data-collection design stage. The analysis of people's propensity to collaborate during data collection is a crucial issue for the application of burdensome techniques. The choice of technique will definitely affect the quality of the collected data and hence the survey outcomes.

Moreover, each technique, or a convenient transformation of it, was associated to a computer-assisted data-collection mode. The more complex techniques (i.e. those based on ranking, pair-comparison of the items or on budget partitioning among the items) are inappropriate for CATI surveys but may be applied in self-administered data-collection modes (CASI, CAWI). In a face-to-face survey, a ranking-based technique may be adopted with the appropriate training of interviewers. The presence of an interviewer may support the administration of paired comparisons or of a reduced type of paired comparisons such as the tournament technique.

The simpler techniques are that of picking the best/worst items and that of rating the items. Let us concentrate on the latter, because many authors advise using it because of its practical simplicity and the validity of the obtainable estimates. If the mechanics of the duties implied by the ranking and rating procedures are compared, it can be concluded that they realise two different aims. Ranking applies to studies whose general aim is to resolve conflicts among the respondents' interests, classifying items and taking decisions, since the inner pattern is measured by the comparative scale of the concerned items. The rating procedure, conversely, enables researchers to elicit the respondents' structural values in an unconstrained manner (Ovada 2004). This difference also applies if paired comparisons and the rating technique are compared (Aloysius et al. 2006). Hence, a rating does not imply a contrast between the items but the "absolute" importance of each item with respect to the subject matter. The rating procedure is inadequate for item classification and decision making, because it is exposed both to social desirability bias and to non-discrimination between the items. The responses obtainable with different techniques may be conditioned by the respondents' culture as far as culture correlates with the task difficulty and responding availability. If the researcher suspects that either the participation level or the quality of responses may depend on people's culture, easier tasks (namely, the rating technique, short lists of alternatives or a qualitative rather a quantitative scale) should be applied. Besides, more research is needed to control the effects of culture-conditioned errors on responses.

Let us consider the case in which ratings are transformed into paired comparisons by considering the non-null contrasts between any two items. An analysis of the dominance matrix constructed with the informative contrasts may give more discriminatory estimates of the items' effective values than those obtainable by processing the observed ratings directly. This trick could overcome the non-differentiation problem, but it is unable to eliminate the social desirability effect (see also Chapman and Staelin 1982; Louvriere et al. 1993).

Even if a technique satisfies the researcher's aims and the context conditions, he or she should consider collecting, and then processing, a combination of data obtained with two or more techniques. A combination of multiple-source data is sometimes called "data enrichment" (Ben-Akiva et al. 1994), because any data-collection technique captures aspects of the choice process for which it is more appropriate.[9] The adoption of either a ranking-based or a picking-the-best/worst technique, before a rating, may induce the respondents to adopt comparative response logics that they generalise to the subsequent rating task, and this may attenuate the effect of anchoring responses to the scale extremes while exposing the respondents to the full range of the possible values before rating the items. McCarty and Shrum (2000) showed that the application of the simple most-least procedure before a rating took one-third more time than usually required by a simple rating procedure.

Research on preference regularity is under way. Regular is a methodological outcome that is common to two or more preference elicitation techniques. Louvriere et al. (2000) applied the regularity criterion to the parameters they estimated and stated that two methods are regular if they exhibit parameters that are equal up to a positive constant. They found that parameter estimates are regular in a surprisingly large number of cases.

In conclusion, a meta-analysis of empirical studies and experiments on real populations would be welcome to shed light on the relationships between the statistical properties and the practical and purpose-related feasibility of techniques. In fact, the results of experiments vary according to contents and contexts. Thus content- and context-specific rules should be determined that are appropriate to survey peculiar segments of the target population. Instead, the experiments conducted on convenience samples, such as on-campus students, which may inform on estimates' validity are irrelevant for both reliability and feasibility judgements on survey techniques.

---

[9] Data-collection techniques alternative to the basic ones presented in Sect. 2 are rare but increasing in number. Louvriere et al. (2000) quote experiments by Meyer (1977), Johnson (1989), Louvriere (1993) and Chrzan (1994).

Acknowledgments This paper was realised thanks to a grant from the Italian Ministry of Education, University and Research (PRIN 2007, CUP C91J11002460001) and another grant from the University of Padua (Ateneo 2008, CUP CPDA081538).

References

Aloysius, J. A., Davis, F. D., Wilson, D. D., Taylor, A. R., & Kottemann, J. E. (2006). User acceptance of multi-criteria decision support systems: The impact of preference elicitation techniques. *European Journal of Operational Research, 169*(1), 273–285.

Alwin, D. F., & Krosnick, J. A. (1985). The measurement of values in surveys: A comparison of ratings and rankings. *Public Opinion Quarterly, 49*(4), 535–552.

Baumgartner, H., & Steenkamp, J.-B. E. M. (2001). Response styles in marketing research: A cross-national investigation. *Journal of Marketing Research, 38*(2), 143–156.

Bassi, F., & Fabbris, L. (1997). Estimators of nonsampling errors in interview-reinterview supervised surveys with interpenetrated assignments. In: L. Lyberg, P. Biemer, M. Collins, E. de Leeuw, C. Dippo, N. Schwarz & D. Trewin (Eds.), *Survey measurement and process quality* (pp. 733–751). New York: Wiley.

Beatty, S. E., Kahle, L. R., Homer, P., & Misra, K. (1985). Alternative measurement approaches to consumer values: The list of values and the Rokeach value survey. *Psychology and Marketing, 2*(3), 81–200.

Ben-Akiva, M. E., Bradley, M., Morikawa, T., Benjamin, J., Novak, T., Oppenwal, H., & Rao, V. (1994). Combining revealed and stated preferences data. *Marketing Letters, 5*(4), 335–351.

Bettman, J. R., Johnson, E. J., Luce, M. F., & Payne, J. (1993). Correlation, conflict, and choice. *Journal of Experimental Psychology, 19*, 931–951.

Bhat, C. (1997). An endogenous segmentation mode choice model with an application to intercity travel. *Transportation Science, 31*(1), 34–48.

Brauer, A. (1957). A new proof of theorems of Perron and Frobenius on nonnegative matrices. *Duke Mathematical Journal, 24*, 367–368.

Brauer, A., & Gentry, I. C. (1968). On the characteristic roots of tournament matrices. *Bulletin of the American Mathematical Society, 74*(6), 1133–1135.

Brunk, H. D. (1960). Mathematical models for ranking from paired comparisons. *Journal of the American Statistical Association, 55*, 503–520.

Cattell, R. B. (1944). Psychological measurement: Normative, ipsative, interactive. *Psychological Review, 51*, 292–303.

Chan, W., & Bentler, P. M. (1993). The covariance structure analysis of ipsative data. *Sociological Methods Research, 22*(2), 214–247.

Chapman, R., & Staelin, R. (1982). Exploiting rank ordered choice set data within the stochastic utility model. *Journal of Marketing Research, 19*(3), 288–301.

Chrzan, K. (1994). Three kinds of order effects in choice-based conjoint analysis. *Marketing Letters, 5*(2), 165–172.

Clemans, W. V. (1966). *An analytical and empirical examination of some properties of ipsative measures. Psychometric monographs* (Vol. 14). Richmond: Psychometric Society. http://www.psychometrika.org/journal/online/MN14.pdf.

Coombs, C. H. (1976). *A theory of data*. Ann Arbor: Mathesis Press.

Conrad, F. G., Couper, M. P., Tourangeau, R., & Galesic, M. (2005). *Interactive feedback can improve the quality of responses in web surveys*. In: ESF Workshop on Internet Survey Methodology (Dubrovnik, 26–28 September 2005).

Crosby, L. A., Bitter, M. J., & Gill, J. D. (1990). Organizational structure of values. *Journal of Business Research, 20*, 123–134.

Cunningham, W. H., Cunningham, I. C. M., & Green, R. T. (1977). The ipsative process to reduce response set bias. *Public Opinion Quarterly, 41*, 379–384.

Elrod, T., Louvriere, J. J., & Davey, K. S. (1993). An empirical comparison of ratings-based and choice-based conjoint models. *Journal of Marketing Research, 24*(3), 368–377.

Fabbris, L. (2010). Dimensionality of scores obtained with a paired-comparison tournament system of questionnaire items. In: F. Palumbo, C. N. Lauro & M. J. Greenacre (Eds.), *Data analysis and classification. Proceedings of the 6th Conference of the Classification and Data Analysis Group of the Società Italiana di Statistica* (pp. 155–162). Berlin: Springer.

Fabbris, L. (2011). One-dimensional preference imputation through transition rules. In: B. Fichet, D. Piccolo, R. Verde & M. Vichi (Eds.), *Classification and multivariate analysis for complex data structures* (pp. 245–252). Heidelberg: Springer.

Fabbris, L., & Fabris, G. (2003). Sistema di quesiti a torneo per rilevare l'importanza di fattori di customer satisfaction mediante un sistema CATI. In: L. Fabbris (Ed.), *LAID-OUT: Scoprire i Rischi Con l'analisi di Segmentazione* (p. 322). Padova: Cleup.

Fellegi, I. (1964). Response variance and its estimation. *Journal of the American Statistical Association, 59*, 1016–1041.

Ganassali, S. (2008). The influence of the design of web survey questionnaires on the quality of responses. *Survey Research Methods, 2*(1), 21–32.

Green, P. E., & Srinivasan, V. (1990). Conjoint analysis in marketing: New developments with implications for research and practice. *Journal of Marketing, 54*(4), 3–19.

Green, P. E., Krieger, A. M., & Wind, Y. (2001). Thirty years of conjoint analysis: Reflections and prospects. *Interfaces, 31*(3.2), 556–573.

Gustafsson, A., Herrmann, A., & Huber, F. (Eds.). (2007). *Conjoint measurement: Methods and applications* (4th edn.). Berlin: Springer.

Harzing, A.-W., et al. (2009). Rating versus ranking: What is the best way to reduce response and language bias in cross-national research? *International Business Review, 18*(4), 417–432.

Hensher, D. A. (1998). Establishing a fare elasticity regime for urban passenger transport: Non-concession commuters. *Journal of Transport Economics and Policy, 32*(2), 221–246.

Jacoby, W. G. (2011). *Measuring value choices: Are rank orders valid indicators?* Presented at the 2011 Annual Meetings of the Midwest Political Science Association, Chicago, IL.

Johnson, R. (1989). Making decisions with incomplete information: The first complete test of the inference model. *Advances in Consumer Research, 16*, 522–528.

Kamakura, W. A., & Mazzon, J. A. (1991). Value segmentation: A model for the measurement of values and value systems. *Journal of Consumer Research, 18*, 208–218.

Kish, L. (1965). *Survey sampling*. New York: Wiley.

Krosnick, J. A., & Alwin, D. F. (1988). A test of the form-resistant correlation hypothesis: Ratings, rankings, and the measurement of values. *Public Opinion Quarterly, 52*(4), 526–538.

Kuhfeld, W. F., Tobias, R. B., & Garratt, M. (1994). Efficient experimental design with marketing research applications. *Journal of Marketing Research, 31*(4), 545–557.

Louvriere, J. J., Fox, M., & Moore, W. (1993). Cross-task validity comparisons of stated preference choice models. *Marketing Letters, 4*(3), 205–213.

Louvriere, J. J., Hensher, D. A., & Swait, J. D. (2000). *Stated choice methods: Analysis and application*. Cambridge: Cambridge University Press.

Maio, G. R., Roese, N. J., Seligman, C., & Katz, A. (1996). Rankings, ratings, and the measurement of values: Evidence for the superior validity of ratings. *Basic and Applied Social Psychology, 18*(2), 171–181.

Martignon, L., & Hoffrage, U. (2002). Fast, frugal, and fit: Simple heuristics for paired comparisons. *Theory and Decisions, 52*, 29–71.

McCarty, J. A., & Shrum, L. J. (1997). Measuring the importance of positive constructs: A test of alternative rating procedures. *Marketing Letters, 8*(2), 239–250.

McCarty, J. A., & Shrum, L. J. (2000). The measurement of personal values in research. *Public Opinion Quarterly, 64*, 271–298.

Meyer, R. (1977). An experimental analysis of student apartment selection decisions under uncertainty. *Great Plains-Rocky Mountains Geographical Journal, 6*(special issue), 30–38.

Moshkovich, H. M., Schellenberger, R. E., & Olson, D. L. (1998). Data influences the result more than preferences: Some lessons from implementation of multiattribute techniques in a real decision task. *Decision Support Systems, 22*, 73–84.

Munson, J. M., & McIntyre, S. H. (1979). Developing practical procedures for the measurement of personal values in cross-cultural marketing. *Journal of Marketing Research, 16*(26), 55–60.

Ovada, S. (2004). Ratings and rankings: Reconsidering the structure of values and their measurement. *International Journal of Social Research Methodology, 7*(5), 404–414.

Rankin, W. L., & Grube, J. W. (1980). A comparison of ranking and rating procedures for value system measurement. *European Journal of Social Psychology, 10*(3), 233–246.

Rokeach, M. (1967). *Value survey.* Sunnyvale: Halgren Tests (873 Persimmon Avenue).

Rokeach, M. (1979). *Understanding human values: Individual and societal.* New York: Free Press.

Rokeach, M., & Ball Rokeach, S. J. (1989). Stability and change in American value priorities. *American Psychologist, 44*, 775–784.

Saaty, T. L. (1977). A scaling method for priorities in hierarchical structures. *Journal of Mathematical Psychology, 15*, 234–281.

Scheffé, H. (1952). An analysis of variance for paired comparisons. *Journal of the American Statistical Association, 47*, 381–400.

Small, K. A., & Rosen, H. S. (1981). Applied welfare economics with discrete choice models. *Econometrica, 49*(1), 105–130.

Swait, J., & Adamowicz, W. (1996). *The effect of choice environment and task demands on consumer behavior: Discriminating between contribution and confusion.* Department of Rural Economy, Staff Paper 96-09, University of Alberta, Alberta.

Vanleeuwen, D. M., & Mandabach, K. H. (2002). A note on the reliability of ranked items. *Sociological Methods Research, 31*(1), 87–105.

Assessing Multi-Item Scales for Subjective Measurement

Cristina Davino and Rosaria Romano

Abstract In this paper a method for assessing different multi-item scales in sub-jective measurement is described and discussed. The method is a combination of analysis of variance models and multivariate techniques. It allows us comparisons among the scales by considering the multivariate information provided by the items. Focus is given on the way individual differences in the use of the scales may be interpreted and crossed with respondent characteristics. The approach is illustrated by analysing data from a survey on the assessment of students' university quality of life.

1 Introduction

Results deriving from a subjective measurement process depend on survey conditions and methodological choices, among them the measurement scale, the nature of the model (one-dimensional or multidimensional), the individual characteristics, the survey plan and the scale features. The present paper refers to single-stimulus data used to measure a single concept through multi-item scales. Such a framework is quite common in all contexts where the phenomenon under investigation cannot be directly measured due to the presence of concurrent factors acting as determinants. In subjective measurement, such elements are composed of a battery of items, a scale, that can be structured according to different choices regarding the scale reference

C. Davino
Department of Studies for Economic Development,
University of Macerata, Macerata, Italy
e-mail: cdavino@unimc.it

R. Romano
Department of Economy and Statistics,
University of Calabria, Arcavacata di Rende (CS), Italy
e-mail: rosaria.romano@unical.it

C. Davino and L. Fabbris (eds.), *Survey Data Collection and Integration*,
DOI: 10.1007/978-3-642-21308-3_3, © Springer-Verlag Berlin Heidelberg 2013

(e.g. an evaluation, a preference, a perception, a judgment) (Maggino and Schifini 2003), the type of information (verbal, numerical, graphical), the width (number of categories for each item). The final goal is to provide a composite index aggregating all the items each of which represents an aspect of the theoretical concept.

The aim of this paper is to assess the differences in the results of the measurement process deriving from the scale features. In particular, the role of single features on the survey results and the effect that derives from alternative scale features are explored while the effect played by the sampling plan is left out.

The assessment of different scales in subjective measurement is performed by proposing a new approach in the theoretical framework of exploratory and confirmatory analysis. The proposal is based on a combination of analysis of variance models (McCulloch and Searle 2001) and multivariate methods (Mardia et al. 1979). This strategy has already been proposed by Endrizzi et al. (2011) in the context of consumers' preferences and by Davino and Romano (2011) in the context of scientific research assessment. The aim of the present work is to adapt such an approach to the subjective measurement framework in order to assess if methodological choices affect the composite index variability and to evaluate differences and relationships among alternative scales. The combination of exploratory and confirmatory methods is an innovative solution based on a multivariate approach where individual differences among the observations are highlighted and graphical tools that aim at enhancing the interpretation of the results are adopted.

2 Subjective Measurement in the Social Sciences

Measurement is crucial to all sciences where it is often necessary to resort to the empirical observation to represent phenomena deriving from a theory. In such a framework, measurement can be defined as "the process of linking abstract concepts to empirical indicants" (Carmines and Zeller 1979), namely it is the result of an interaction between the theory and the empirical observation (Marradi 1981).

In social sciences, the measurement generally involves subjective evaluations and it is necessary to define a continuum along which the respondent puts him/her scores. It is a matter of fact that subjective measurement would require ratio scales but the use of interval or even ordinal scales is very common.

The result of the measurement process depends on several choices adopted by the researcher:

- the first issue regards the *type of data* to be observed (Coombs 1964; Fabbris 2012): preference data (objects ranked or scored according to some criterion), single-stimulus data (subjects respond to stimuli one at a time), stimulus comparison data (subjects have to choose, from a set of stimuli, the one that has more or less a specific attribute), similarity data (subjects are asked to choose from pairs of stimuli according to a predefined criterion).

- The *one-dimensional* or *multidimensional* nature of the concept to be measured leads to a unidimensional or multidimensional model (Sullivan 1979). The measurement process is often realised through a *multi-item* scale because a complex theoretical concept rarely is fully represented by a *single item* (McIver 1981; Bergkvist and Rossiter 2007).
- *Individual characteristics* (Romano et al. 2008) and the *survey plan* can also influence the obtained results.
- *Scale features* have an important role too. In particular, the *scale reference* depends on the concept to be measured and it can be, for example, an evaluation, a preference, a perception or a judgment. Scales can also be distinguished according to the selected *type* (verbal, numerical, graphical) and each choice involves both pros and cons. Verbal scales divide the continuum in parts defined by verbal labels so that preferences are expressed on an ordinal scale and a quantification of the verbal scales (direct or indirect) should be required a posteriori. A typical ordinal scale is the well known Likert scale, which uses, as evaluation criterion, the degree of agreement or disagreement. In verbal scales it is not possible to guarantee that interviewees perceive the same distance among the verbal labels. Numerical scales divide the continuum in segments defined by numbers so that semantic interpretation problems are avoided. A graphical scale which is used quite often is the anchoring scale (also applied to interval scales) through which a continuum is proposed to respondents and an arbitrary partition of the continuum is defined a posteriori. The setting of a scale is finalised when the number of categories (*width*) is defined, which means, in case of a verbal scale the number of verbal labels, for a numerical scale the number of proposed scores and for an anchoring scale the number of classes in which the continuum is discretised. The scientific debate about the optimal range of a scale is lively and concerns mainly the choice between either a small or a large number, or an even or odd number of categories.

The previous remarks about subjective choices required by the measurement process highlight that a posteriori analysis of the obtained results is advisable. To this end, several contributions in literature (Osterlind 1983; Gilbert 1993; Maggino 2003; Maggino and Schifini 2003) have been devoted to measuring differences in the use of multi-item scales but they are mainly based on univariate or at most bivariate comparisons among alternatives scales.

3 An Empirical Analysis: Assessing Students' University Quality of Life

3.1 The Survey

The empirical reference framework is represented by the assessment of the students' university quality of life. A survey has been conducted on a sample of students attending at least the second year of classes at the Faculty of Economics (University of Macerata, Italy). A quota sampling scheme is used with *gender* and *year of attendance* as stratification variables. A questionnaire is submitted to each respondent by means of face to face interviews. Besides information on age, course and aptitude for studying, each respondent is asked to rate his or her degree of satisfaction on three different dimensions of the students' university quality of life: *didactics features, services and infrastructures, relationships with other students*. For the purpose of this paper only the section related to the *didactics features* is considered; it is measured by a multi-item scale composed of the following six items:

- availability of the teacher out-of-class/in-class (D1);
- teaching ability (D2);
- exam planning (D3);
- heavy workload (D4);
- clarity in lecturing (D5);
- schedule of the course (D6).

Each respondent is asked to provide the degree of satisfaction on the six items using four different types of scales: verbal evaluation (5 points), numerical judgment (10 points), graphical judgment (10 points) and graphical judgment (5 points). The four types of questions derive from some combinations of scale features: *reference* (evaluation or judgment),[1] *type* (verbal, numerical, graphical), *width* (5 or 10 points). The verbal scale has been observed on a five-level ordinal scale (from definitely agree to definitely disagree) but before the analysis phase a direct quantification is used by assigning to its categories scores from 1 to 5 as it is usually done with a Likert scale.

3.2 Univariate and Bivariate Analysis

The study of the different scale performance is pursued through two types of comparisons: *within scale comparison* and *between scale comparison*. In the first case, simple bar charts are used to graphically represent the distributions of the different categories inside the same scale. In the second case, both univariate and bivariate descriptive statistics are used to compare scales.

Figures 1 and 2 show a similar use of the *10point* scale. In fact, on both the graphical and numerical scales there is a high degree of satisfaction and a regular use of all the categories. In addition, the numerical scale presents an overestimation of the satisfaction due to a frequent selection of the higher categories. The *5point* scales present a similar pattern among them as well. The related bar charts in Figs. 3 and 4 show that respondents seldom selected the extreme categories and often declared a medium-to-high degree of satisfaction.

A first between scale comparison is based on some basic univariate descriptive statistics presented in Table 1 where results are grouped according to the scale width

---

[1] A verbal evaluation scale has the degree of agreement or disagreement as categories while for a verbal judgment scale categories are degrees from positive to negative.

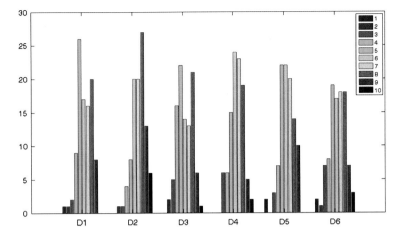

Fig. 1 *Judgment-graphical-10point* scale bar charts

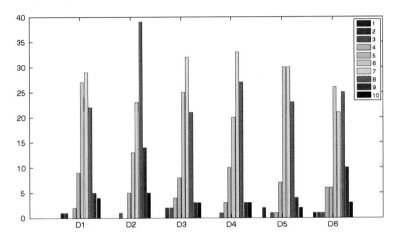

Fig. 2 *Judgment-numerical-10point* scale bar charts

(for each item, the final number represents the number of categories). It is obvious that comparisons according to the mean values only make sense in the case that the compared scales have the same number of categories. Evaluations about skewness and variability prescind from the width of the scale. A similarity between *judgment-graphical-5point* scale and the *evaluation-verbal-5point* scale on both the average values and the variability coefficients is evident. On the other hand the *judgment-numerical-10point* scale differs from the *judgment-graphical-10point* scale since the former presents average values always greater than the latter while variability coefficients result higher in the latter. The *judgment-numerical-10point* and *evaluation-verbal-5point* scales present a high degree of skewness, and this indicates a more frequent use of the higher categories.

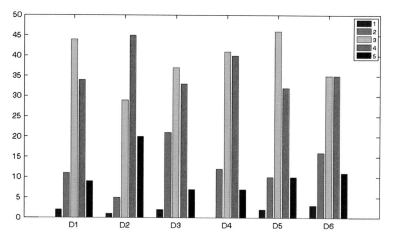

Fig. 3 *Judgment-graphical-5point* scale bar charts

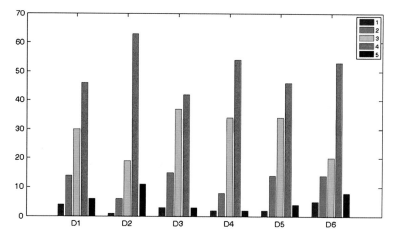

Fig. 4 *Evaluation-verbal-5point* scale bar charts

The analysis of the correlations between each couple of items on the four different scales are reported in Table 2. The correlations are generally high, thus indicating a good agreement between responses. The similarity between the two graphical scales is the most outstanding result while the verbal scale seems to be the most separate one. Such results confirm our hypothesis that the results of the measurement process are related to the scale features.

Table 1 Univariate descriptive statistics on the observed sample

Variable	Mean	Standard deviation	Skewness (Fisher)	Variability coefficient
D1 – evaluation-verbal-5	3.36	0.93	−0.63	0.28
D2 – evaluation-verbal-5	3.77	0.76	−0.97	0.20
D3 – evaluation-verbal-5	3.27	0.86	−0.56	0.26
D4 – evaluation-verbal-5	3.46	0.75	−1.00	0.22
D5 – evaluation-verbal-5	3.36	0.84	−0.57	0.25
D6 – evaluation-verbal-5	3.45	0.99	−0.82	0.29
D1 – judgment-graphical-5	3.37	0.87	−0.15	0.26
D2 – judgment-graphical-5	3.78	0.86	−0.43	0.23
D3 – judgment-graphical-5	3.22	0.92	−0.07	0.29
D4 – judgment-graphical-5	3.42	0.79	−0.04	0.23
D5 – judgment-graphical-5	3.38	0.87	−0.09	0.26
D6 – judgment-graphical-5	3.35	0.97	−0.23	0.29
D1 – judgment-graphical-10	6.21	1.69	−0.27	0.27
D2 – judgment-graphical-10	7.14	1.61	−0.48	0.23
D3 – judgment-graphical-10	6.00	1.82	−0.01	0.30
D4 – judgment-graphical-10	6.39	1.59	−0.23	0.25
D5 – judgment-graphical-10	6.23	1.70	−0.43	0.27
D6 – judgment-graphical-10	6.17	1.94	−0.33	0.32
D1 – judgment-numerical-10	6.82	1.47	−0.66	0.22
D2 – judgment-numerical-10	7.55	1.26	−0.56	0.17
D3 – judgment-numerical-10	6.65	1.49	−0.64	0.22
D4 – judgment-numerical-10	6.89	1.30	−0.27	0.19
D5 – judgment-numerical-10	6.74	1.43	−1.17	0.21
D6 – judgment-numerical-10	6.83	1.64	−0.72	0.24

4 An Innovative Multivariate Approach

In the following, a new approach is proposed to compare the scales to one another taking their multivariate structure into account.

The main idea is that a multi-item scale can be used to measure a complex concept and that the single items represent a set of observed indicators aimed at measuring such a concept. In our example there are six items composing the *didactics features* concept. In general, a unique index is obtained by synthesizing individual indicators (quantitative/qualitative measures observed on a set of units). Several approaches could be followed to synthesize a group of indicators.

In this paper, responses to the six items in the four multi-item scales are averaged for each respondent. Even if the adopted synthesis method could be considered naive compared to more advanced ones (for example, structural models), it has been used because the aim of the paper is not to discuss differences among methods to synthesize indicators but to describe the potentiality of the proposed multivariate approach in assessing different scales in subjective measurements.

52   C. Davino and R. Romano

Table 2 Bivariate descriptive statistics on the observed sample

	D1eval-ver-5	D1jud-gra-5	D1jud-num-10	D1jud-gra-10
D1eval-ver-5	1.00	0.74	0.80	0.71
D1jud-gra-5	0.74	1.00	0.82	0.95
D1jud-num-10	0.80	0.82	1.00	0.81
D1jud-gra-10	0.71	0.95	0.81	1.00
	D2eval-ver-5	D2jud-gra-5	D2jud-num-10	D2jud-gra-10
D2eval-ver-5	1.00	0.63	0.73	0.63
D2jud-gra-5	0.63	1.00	0.79	0.95
D2jud-num-10	0.73	0.79	1.00	0.77
D2jud-gra-10	0.63	0.95	0.77	1.00
	D3eval-ver-5	D3jud-gra-5	D3jud-num-10	D3jud-gra-10
D3eval-ver-5	1.00	0.61	0.64	0.62
D3jud-gra-5	0.61	1.00	0.72	0.96
D3jud-num-10	0.64	0.72	1.00	0.70
D3jud-gra-10	0.62	0.96	0.70	1.00
	D4eval-ver-5	D4jud-gra-5	D4jud-num-10	D4jud-gra-10
D4eval-ver-5	1.00	0.57	0.73	0.61
D4jud-gra-5	0.57	1.00	0.71	0.94
D4jud-num-10	0.73	0.71	1.00	0.70
D4jud-gra-10	0.61	0.94	0.70	1.00
	D5eval-ver-5	D5jud-gra-5	D5jud-num-10	D5jud-gra-10
D5eval-ver-5	1.00	0.66	0.76	0.66
D5jud-gra-5	0.66	1.00	0.79	0.95
D5jud-num-10	0.76	0.79	1.00	0.80
D5jud-gra-10	0.66	0.95	0.80	1.00
	D6eval-ver-5	D6jud-gra-5	D6jud-num-10	D6jud-gra-10
D6eval-ver-5	1.00	0.67	0.83	0.72
D6jud-gra-5	0.67	1.00	0.84	0.96
D6jud-num-10	0.83	0.84	1.00	0.88
D6jud-gra-10	0.72	0.96	0.88	1.00

Having obtained a composite index, the proposed approach consists in applying a multi-step procedure based on a combination of mixed model analysis of variance models (McCulloch and Searle 2001) and multivariate methods (Mardia et al. 1979) for analysing differences among the obtained indexes. The proposed approach has the advantage of providing comparisons among different multi-item scales considering the multivariate information provided by each single item inside the scale.

An additional feature of the approach consists in including in such comparison also the analysis of additional information usually related to the respondents' socio-demographic variables. This procedure permits to investigate if an eventual response is also related to specific characteristics of respondents.

Table 3 Anova factors and levels

Factors	Levels
Reference	Evaluation
	Judgment
Type	Verbal-5point
	Numerical-10point
	Graphical-5point
	Graphical-10point

4.1 The Methodology

The proposed strategy consists of three steps:

1. synthesis of the multi-item scale into a unique index;
2. evaluation of the scale differences and the external information through analysis of variance (ANOVA);
3. exploration of individual differences in the use of scales through principal component analysis (PCA).

The first step consists of building a single index from the different items of each scale. The synthesis is obtained by computing the simple average across different items. In order to ease the comparisons among the four indexes, they have been normalised to vary in the interval 0-1. The used normalisation, known as Min-Max normalisation, is realised by subtracting from each indicator its minimum value and dividing by its width. This normalisation allows to remove the problem of analysing indicators measured on a different width to be removed.

ANOVA is a very useful method when the objective is to assess the impact of some controllable factors (categorical variables) on a specific response (continuous variable). The impact is significant if the variability *between* the groups defined by the factor levels (categories) is much larger than the variability *within* the groups. An ANOVA model is equivalent to a linear model where the response variable becomes the dependent variable, and each factor is transformed into a *dummy variable* according to the number of levels.

In our example the dependent variables are the indexes obtained from the first step, one for each type of scale. The factors are the categorical variables characterising the different scales. Table 3 provides a description of the different factors and levels considered in the study. The factor named *type* covers both the type and the width scale features described in Sect. 2. The *gender* factor is considered as external information in the study.

Let $\mathbf{X}$ ($N \times P$) be the matrix of the P indices observed on the N students and *reference (r)* and *type (t)* the two main factors, respectively with $I = 2$ and $J = 4$ levels. The *students* factor s will consist of as many levels as the number of respondents and it is nested in the *external information* factor *gender (g)*, with $M = 2$ levels. A factor is nested when subgroups of units match only one of the levels of the nesting factor and not each one of them, as it usually happens in a crossed design. The *full* ANOVA model can then be written as:

$$y_{ijmn} = \mu + r_i + t_j(r) + g_m + s_n(g) + e_{ijmn} \tag{1}$$

where y_{ijmn} is the nth observation obtained using the ith ($i = 1, \ldots I$) level of the r factor and the jth ($j = 1, \ldots J$) level of the t factor and considering the mth level of the g factor. In model (1), the general mean is represented by μ, while r and t are the main effects, with *reference* being the nesting factor of *type*. All these factors are considered fixed. The main effect of the factor represented by the students and nested in the external information factor g is s_n. Finally, the term e_{ijmn} is the random error. As the considered units can be viewed as one specific 'sample' of the whole population of statistical units, the related factor is a random factor. An ANOVA model including both fixed and random factors is called Mixed Model ANOVA (McCulloch and Searle 2001).

Model (1) corresponds to a simultaneous ANOVA for all statistical units and it is estimated by stacking in a pile the same matrix containing the different combinations of factor levels and the corresponding indices obtained for each statistical unit. This type of data modeling permits to estimate all relevant main effects and then model the individual differences among the units. Note that not all possible combinations of factor levels are considered since the type factor is nested in the reference one. In fact the *verbal-5point* level of the *type* factor only goes with the evaluation level of the *reference* factor while all the other *type* levels match only the judgment level of the *reference* factor.

Results from model (1) show which factors mostly contribute to the differences among the scales and also the impact of these effects on each respondent.

In order to explore such differences and similarities among the units, a PCA exploiting all the advantages of the factorial methods is performed on the residuals of a reduced ANOVA model without the *student* factor.

A study of the differences among the units in the use of the scales is already achieved by introducing the *student* effect as an additive factor in the *full* ANOVA (Model 1). In fact, the main effect plot shows graphically such differences. In the case of many statistical units this plot is unreadable and more sophisticated exploratory methods are required. Principal Component Analysis is appropriate for this aim since it allows us to synthesize multivariate data in a few linear combinations to be plotted by means of factorial planes. Specifically, individual differences will be explored by a PCA on the residuals obtained in a *reduced* ANOVA model without the *student* main factor:

$$y_{ijmn} = \mu + r_i + t_j(r) + g_m + e_{ijmn} \tag{2}$$

Residuals from this second model contain information on individual differences among students with respect to the scale factors plus the random error.

In order to run the PCA on the residuals from model (2), these have to be rearranged in a data matrix with the units as rows and the indices, corresponding to the different

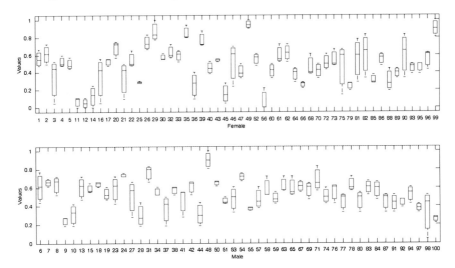

Fig. 5 Boxplot of the different indexes for each respondent

synthesis of the multi-items scales, as columns. Due to the nested design only four different combinations of factors levels are possible thus providing a very simple data matrix.

The impact of the external information is investigated by including it in the PCA as a supplementary variable and projecting it onto the factorial planes obtained by the residuals from model (2).

The proposed PCA on the reduced ANOVA residuals allows us to obtain information on the effect of units on the different scales features after the overall mean is removed.

4.2 Main Results

The assessment of the indices obtained using the different scales is explored by means of boxplots grouping the units according to *gender*. Figure 5 shows a higher variability of the female group compared to the male one. In fact several female respondents present larger boxes, which means that women use the scales in a way that differs from men. In addition, the former use a wider width of the scale whereas the latter concentrate their evaluations in the range [0.2-0.8]. This assessment provides only information on the variability of the indices without highlighting the role of the scale features.

Results from the *full* ANOVA model in (1) presented in Table 4 permit to investigate differences in the use of the scales according to the different factors of interest. Results show significant differences both for the *reference* and the *type* factors. These results can be further investigated by Fig. 6 showing the average values of the indices

Table 4 Anova full model

Source	Sum sq.	d.f.	Mean sq.	F	Prob>F
Student(gender)	12.5693	98	0.12826	17.20	0.0000
Reference	0.4048	1	0.40478	54.29	0.0000
Type(reference)	0.7229	2	0.36146	48.48	0.0000
Gender	0.3398	1	0.33985	2.65	0.1068
Error	2.2145	297	0.00746		
Total	16.2513	399			

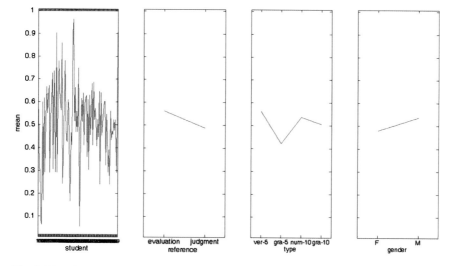

Fig. 6 Plot of Anova means

according to the different levels. As it can be seen, respondents provide lower degrees of satisfaction if they use the *judgment* reference. According to the *type* factor, there exists a large variation inside the 5*point* scales. In particular, the *graphical-5point* scale produces the lowest index values, whereas the *verbal-5point* one the highest. There is no significant effect for the external information, which means that differences brought out from the boxplots cannot be generalised to the population. The *unit* factor points out individual differences between respondents in their values and in their behavior with respect to the different scales. These individual differences are further analysed in the second step of the proposed approach,which consists of exploring residuals from the *reduced* ANOVA model (2).

Loading and score plot from PCA on *reduced* ANOVA residuals are shown in Figs. 7 and 8. The explained variance for the first two components is 95 %. The first component is strongly related to the degree of satisfaction. On the right side of the plot we find students who are very satisfied whatever the type of scale they use, whereas the dissatisfied are positioned on the left hand side. The second component is related to a different use of the scales: positive values are related to higher degrees of satisfaction due to the use of the *verbal-5point* and *numerical-10point* scales and negative values

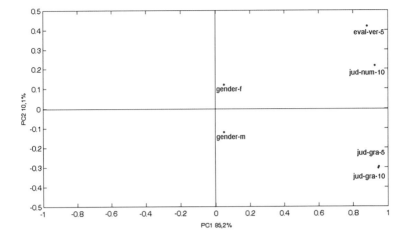

Fig. 7 PCA variables factorial plane

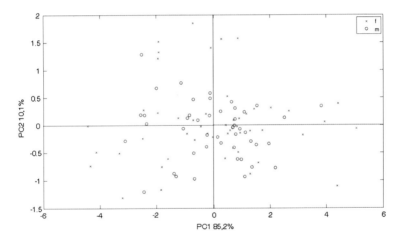

Fig. 8 PCA units factorial plane

relate to higher levels of satisfaction due to the use of the *graphical* scales. The *gender* variable also provides interesting information on the second component. As it can be seen both from the loading and the score plot, the female respondents are those more sensitive to the *verbal-5point* and *numerical-10point* scales, whereas males are more reactive to the graphical scales.

5 Concluding Remarks and Further Developments

The paper has shown the importance of investigating differences in the use of different multi-item scales by respondents during a survey.

The use of simple descriptive statistics have shown differences in scales' features while the introduction of a new multivariate approach has highlighted differences in the use of scales among the respondents and also permitted to relate this different behavior to additional respondent's characteristics.

Further developments may include the testing of additional scale features and the analysis of more complex phenomena requiring a partition in more than one dimension (for example the measurement of university quality of life satisfaction considering all the sections of the questionnaire). Finally, a study for the assessment of the stability of the multivariate results could be carried out to quantify the degree of sensitivity of each unit to the factor level combinations.

References

Bergkvist, L., & Rossiter, J. R. (2007). The predictive validity of multiple-item versus single-item measures of the same constructs. *Journal of Marketing Research XLIV*, 175–184.

Carmines, E. G., & Zeller, R. A. (1979). *Reliability and validity assessment*. Quantitative Applications in the Social Sciences, 17. Newbury Park: SAGE Publications Inc.

Coombs, C. H. (1964). *A theory of data*. New York: Wiley.

Davino, C., & Romano, R. (2011). Exploring the sensitivity of scientific research activity evaluation models by multivariate data analysis. In *Book of Short Papers of the 8th Scientific Meeting of the Classification and Data Analysis Group. Pavia, Italy 7–9 Sept 2011*.

Endrizzi, I., Menichelli, E.: Blling Johansen, S., Veflen Olsen, N., & Naes, T. (2011). Handling of individual differences in rating-based conjoint analysis. *Food Quality and Preference 22*, 241–254.

Fabbris, L. (2012). Measurement scales for scoring or ranking sets of interrelated items. In C. Davino & L. Fabbris (Eds.), *Survey data collection and integration*, pp. 21–44. Heidelberg: Springer.

Gilbert, N. (1993). *Researching social life*. London: Sage.

Maggino, F. (2003). Method Effect in the Measurement of Subjective Dimensions. http://eprints.unifi.it/archive/00000299/.

Maggino, F., & Schifini D'Andrea, S. (2003). Different scales for different survey methods: validation in measuring quality of university life. In M.J. Sirgy, D. Rahtz, & J. Samli (Eds.), *Advances in quality of life research*, pp. 233–256. Dordrecht: Kluwer Academic Publisher.

Mardia, K. V., Kent, J. T., & Bibby, J. M. (1979). *Multivariate analysis*. London: Academic Press.

Marradi, A. (1981). Misurazione e scale: qualche riflessione e una proposta. *Quaderni di Sociol, XXIX* 4, 595–639.

McCulloch, C. E., & Searle, S. R. (2001). *Generalized, linear, and mixed models*. New York: Wiley.

McIver, J. P., & Carmines, E. G. (1981). *Unidimensional scaling*. Sage University Papers Series, Quantitative Applications in the Social Sciences, series no. 07–024. Newbury Park: Sage Publications, Inc.

OECD/JRC. (2008). *Handbook on constructing composite indicators. Methodology and user guide*. Paris: OECD Publishing.

Osterlind, S. J. (1983). *Test item Bias*. Sage University Paper Series on Quantitative Applications in the Social Sciences, SERIES NO. 07–030. Newbury Park: Sage Publications, Inc.

Romano, R., Brockhoff, P. B., Hersleth, M., Tomic, O., & Naes, T. (2008). Correcting for different use of the scale and the need for further analysis of individual differences in sensory analysis. *Food Quality Preference, 19,* 197–209 (2008).

Searle, S. R. (1997). *Linear models.* USA: Wiley Classic Library.

Sullivan, J. L., & Feldman, S. (1979). *Multiple indicators: an introduction.* Sage University Papers Series, Quantitative Applications in the Social Sciences, series no. 07–015. Newbury Park: Sage Publications, Inc.

Statistical Tools in the Joint Analysis of Closed and Open-Ended Questions

Simona Balbi and Nicole Triunfo

Abstract The paper aims at presenting some statistical exploratory methods useful in the joint analysis of data collected in a survey, by means of closed and open-ended questions. After a quick review of the main steps necessary for transforming texts in a numerical table, we focus our attention on Lexical Correspondence Analysis. This method is a popular technique for analysing a lexical table obtained by cross-classifying respondents and free responses. As our interest is often in measuring and visualising the association between socio-demographic characteristics and lexical behaviour, the modalities of one or more closed-ended questions are used both for aggregating individuals similar with respect to the considered variables and reducing the sparseness of the lexical table. Dealing with textual data, the effectiveness of a non symmetrical variant of correspondence analysis is introduced. Furthermore, the advantages of asking a free description of the desired product in a conjoint analysis questionnaire is shown, by applying a factorial conjoint analysis with the lexical table as external information.

1 Introduction

In survey methodology, the use and the implication of closed and open-ended questions in a questionnaire is interesting both in terms of cognitive and practical reasons. Our aim is to illustrate some exploratory statistical methods useful in combining data with different coding systems. The analytic frame is given by Textual Data Analysis (TDA) (Lebart et al. 1991). Here we focus our attention on a usual situation in surveys: we have many closed-ended questions and few open-ended questions. Therefore the

S. Balbi (✉) · N. Triunfo
Department of Mathematics and Statistics,University of Naples Federico II, Naples, Italy
e-mail: simona.balbi@unina.it

N. Triunfo
e-mail: nicole.triunfo@unina.it

C. Davino and L. Fabbris (eds.), *Survey Data Collection and Integration*,
DOI: 10.1007/978-3-642-21308-3_4, © Springer-Verlag Berlin Heidelberg 2013

corresponding database consists both in numerical fields (usually related to categorical variables) and in alphanumeric fields (related to strings, expressed in natural language), whose destiny is often to be discarded or transformed in numeric variables by post-categorisation. This last procedure may cause non-sampling errors and drawbacks from a statistical viewpoint.

In the following we show some statistical methods and strategies for avoiding this loss of information and for emphasizing the interest of answers given in an open format. First of all, we present the classical method, Lexical Correspondence Analysis, with a variation introduced in order to take into account the different role played by categorical and textual variables (Balbi 1995). Then, showing the advantages obtained by introducing a textual table as external information in a conjoint analysis experiment (Balbi et al. 2008).

2 Textual Data Analysis

Many research fields have "studying language" as the main topic. From a quantitative viewpoint, TDA is strictly connected with the *French School of Multidimensional Data Analysis*", which aims at finding homogeneities and peculiarities in linguistic behaviors. The methodological tools are given by multivariate descriptive techniques, usually applied to observational data. The output consists in identifying an underlying latent structure able to synthesize information and to give graphical representations in order to highlight the semantic connections in the textual data base. TDA often consists in using well-known methods developed for numerical data, in an innovative way, able to treat peculiar problems related to dealing with "very qualitative" data, i.e. words and documents. The pre-processing step can strongly affect results. It is straightforward that the coding and weighting systems are crucial for the analysis (Bolasco 2005), as we shall see in the following. Furthermore, the data matrix is high dimensional and sparse. Therefore attention is given to the development of methods, algorithms and software for analysing these peculiar matrices, known as lexical tables.

3 Pre-Processing and Choosing a Proper Coding and Weighting System in TDA

During the last century, the purpose for studying documental archives from a quantitative viewpoint has changed. The linguistic approach, i.e. the search of regularities in a corpus, was substituted by a lexical approach, i.e. the search about how words are used. In the second half of the century, the lexical-textual analysis introduces the notion of "ambiguity". Nowadays, the text mining analysis focuses on the algorithmic component of problems. New strategies and software have been developed, defining standard procedures for transforming the collection of documents, i.e. the corpus, in a structured data base. Tools developed in natural language processing are useful in this step, because the elementary units of the analysis (e.g. lemmas, stems, types) are not univocally definable and the choice strongly affects the variability and the relations among units. The information about the content of the analysed corpus strongly depends on the pre-processing and coding choices. The basic procedure consists of the following steps: parsing, normalising, tagging. For parsing, the corpus is scanned, identifying the alphabetic characters with the role of separators. In the normalisation step the text is cleaned in order to avoid problematic situations, like e.g. duplications generated by peculiar entities (dates, numbers, acronyms, etc., written in different formats), or names, toponyms, derived by other alphabets. Moreover, it is possible tagging the text with meta-information, such as grammar categories or semantic information. Statistics on the distributions of the lexical parts-of-speech (nouns, verbs, adjectives) and on the functional parts-of-speech (articles, adverbs. . .), or related to the length of sentences, and so on can give a first glance to the corpus. At the end of this procedure, the vocabulary is built, by identifying the elementary units for the analysis.

Sometimes it can be useful to introduce lower and/or upper thresholds on the frequencies, or to delete non content-bearing words, like functional parts-of-speech. On the other side, it is often important to add new units as "repeated segments", i.e. sets of words occurring together with a frequency higher than a predefined threshold. TDA chooses to represent the text with no reference to its organisation in terms of discourse, and the order and the context in which words occur.

In the geometrical approach, characteristic of the "French School of Multidimensional Data Analysis", documents are seen as vectors in the space spanned by words (and vice versa). It is worth noting that the Vector Space Model in Information retrieval adopts a similar viewpoint, with the so called "bag-of-words" coding system. Each document is represented as a vector $d_j = (w_{1j}, w_{2j}, \ldots, w_{Vj})$ in the V-dimensional space spanned by words, V being the number of words in the vocabulary of the analysed corpus. Each elements w_{ij} is the weight of the ith word in the jth document. In TDA w_{ij} is usually the frequency of the word in the document although other measures and normalisations have been proposed, mainly in a text mining frame.

4 Correspondence Analysis

Correspondence Analysis (CA) (Benzecri 1973) is a well-known method, proposed for descriptive purposes in order to synthesize and visualise the association between two categorical variables, respectively with I and J categories. Let be:

- $\mathbf{N}(I, J)$ the contingency table, $[n_{ij}]$ ($i = 1, \ldots, I$ and $j = 1, \ldots, J$)
- $\mathbf{F}(I, J)$ the relative frequency matrix, $[f_{ij} = n_{ij}/n]$, $[n = \sum_i \sum_j n_{ij}]$
- $\mathbf{D}_I(I, I)$ the diagonal matrix of $[f_{i.}]$ row-marginal frequency

- $\mathbf{D}_J(J, J)$ the diagonal matrix of $[f_{.j}]$ column-marginal frequency
- $\mathbf{D}_I^{-1}\mathbf{F}(I, J)$ row-profile matrix, $[f_{ij}/f_{i.}]$
- $\mathbf{FD}_J^{-1}(I, J)$ column-profile matrix, $[f_{ij}/f_{.j}]$

As a matter of fact, profiles are conditional distributions, geometrically represented by points in a multidimensional space. The aim of CA is to represent distances between couples of profile-points in a low dimensional readable space. In
order to obtain a graphical representation, we need to identify a sub-space as close
as possible to the profile-points so that their projections onto this sub-space are their
best (in a least square sense) approximations. Such transformation can be performed
in the space spanned by the row categories, or in the space spanned by the column
categories, inside the so called "duality scheme". The row and column analyses are
equivalent: the same association measure is decomposed (Pearson's ϕ^2), the same
number of dimensions are obtained, and the same quantity of information is lost.
As in many multivariate analysis techniques, the algebraic tool is given by Eckart
and Young's (1936) singular value decomposition (SVD), where peculiar ortho-
normalising constraints on singular vectors are introduced. These constraints relate
to the way CA computes distances. Instead of computing usual Euclidean distances,
i.e.:

$$d_2^2(i, i') = \sum_j (x_{ij} - x_{i'j})^2. \tag{1}$$

being x_{ij} and $x_{i'j}$ the measurements of p variables ($j = 1, \ldots, p$) on two individuals
i and i', CA uses the so-called χ^2 distance that is Euclidean distance standardised
with the marginal frequencies:

$$d_{\chi^2}^2(i, i') = \sum_j (1/f_{.j})(f_{ij}/f_{i.} - f_{i'j}/f_{i'.})^2 \tag{2}$$

and, correspondingly,

$$d_{\chi^2}^2(j, j') = \sum_i (1/f_{i.})(f_{ij}/f_{.j}) - (f_{ij'}/f_{.j'})^2. \tag{3}$$

It allows to jointly represent row-points and column-points on the same plot (CA
joint plot). We introduce just some recalls in order to go back to Lexical Correspondence Analysis (LCA). It is necessary to start from the distributional equivalency
property, which states that if two profiles are equal, merging them in a unique row
(column), with weight being the sum of individual weights, does not alter distances
between columns (rows), and vice versa. This can be useful, for example, when we
are not sure if two words are synonyms. One evident issue of the use of the χ^2-metrics
on the factorial map is a zoom effect for rare categories as $(f_{.j}) \le 1$, and $(f_{i.}) \le 1$.

Fig. 1 The steps of lexical correspondence analysis

4.1 Lexical Correspondence Analysis

One of the ordinary ways for the joint analysis of closed and open-ended questions is LCA (Lebart et al. 1991). The peculiar aim of LCA consists in synthesizing and visualising the association (and opposition) between words in order to explore the content of a corpus (Fig. 1).

Dealing with survey data, the corpus consists of the answers given by interviewees to one (or more) open-ended question(s). The data structure is the so called lexical table obtained by cross-classifying respondents by words, and it is assumed to be a contingency table. Consequently, it can be analysed by means of CA. Preliminarily, the pre-processing step has to be performed and LCA is characterised by some standard choices. In LCA tradition the columns of the lexical table are the "graphical" forms, defined as "the sequence of characters delimited by special characters (separators)". Usually neither grammatic tagging nor semantic tagging are performed and normalisation is limited to transform upper cases in lower cases. Sometimes it is helpful to consider thresholds for frequencies and introduce repeated segments as elementary units. The main reason against a deep pre-processing is that it can alter the freedom of respondents. The idea is that we choose the open-ended questions, because we want to obtain as much information as possible and the way respondents freely communicate their own thoughts contains additional information. On the one hand, this is the easiest (and inexpensive) way of building the lexical table and it gives the possibility to perform a language-independent analysis. On the other hand, this choice affects results, as all ambiguities (homographies, polisemies, etc.) are ignored.

Let $\mathbf{T}$ (n, V) be the lexical table respondents-by-words, with n the number of respondents and V the number of different words in the corpus, i.e. the dimension of the vocabulary. $\mathbf{T}$ is a sparse matrix, with many elements equal to 0. In a statistical analysis, the individual behaviour is usually uninteresting, and we want to study the association between variables. We are more interested in the lexical behavior of "young people" or "old women", instead of Mr/Ms Jones' opinion. We have to combine textual information with the answers given to closed-ended questions. In other terms, we are interested in grouping respondents according to the category they belong to.

Let $\mathbf{Q}(n, G)$ be the indicator matrix containing the answers of our n respondents to a closed question having G categories ($G \ll n$). We obtain the aggregated lexical table $\mathbf{Z}(V, G)$ by the product:

$$\mathbf{Z} = \mathbf{Q'T}. \tag{4}$$

If we consider more than one closed question, we refer to the corresponding compound variable in building the indicator matrix. $\mathbf{Z}$ cross-classifies words and groups of respondents, obtained by considering usually (but not necessarily) socio-demographic variables, e.g. age, or gender, or age-by-gender. Therefore, the general element of $\mathbf{Z}[z_{ig}]$ is the frequency of the ith word ($i = 1, \ldots, V$) in the gth group ($g = 1, \ldots, G$).

Let us consider a small example. During the Nineties, Balbi (1995) collected the advertisements on Italian wines, published on *Il Gambero Rosso,* a magazine for gourmets. The hypothesis to be explored was that Italian regions presented different images for their own products. Starting from the aggregated lexical table cross-classifying regions by words, we obtained the first factorial plan in Fig. 2 by LCA, using the software SPAD. First of all, it is interesting to remind some rules in reading LCA factorial plans, referring to the analysis performed on an aggregated lexical table, categories-by-words. The interpretation of a LCA solution is based on the following rules:

1. the dispersion of points around the origin measured by ϕ^2 shows how strong is the association structure in the table;
2. if two words are closed they are similarly used;
3. if two categories are closed they use a similar vocabulary;
4. if a word and a category are on the map, we cannot directly measure their distance (they belong to two different spaces);
5. the importance of a category/word in the analysis depends both on its coordinate and frequency.

By reading Fig. 2, some interesting results emerge. On the first axis (14.6 % of the whole association structure), the larger agricultural regions, namely *Emilia Romagna* and *Veneto* show a net of producers (*enoteca, regionale*), while on the other side *Marche* and *Abruzzo* refer to individual producers (*colle, castello, suo*). The second axis (13.4 %) opposes gastronomy (*arrosto, selvaggina*) to ideal references (*amore, passione*), supporting the original thesis on different marketing images.

At a first glance, the reader should be surprised by the fact that the most famous Italian producers of wine, i.e. *Piemonte* and *Toscana*, two regions that produce famous wines are not in a distinctive position on the map. Moreover, infrequent words appear. As a consequence, a different way of representing the association in a lexical table by Correspondence Analysis has been proposed.

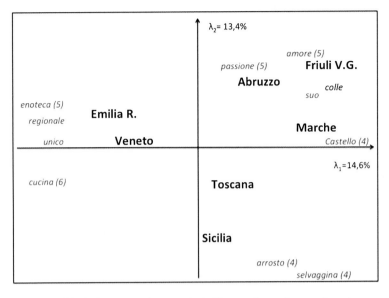

Fig. 2 Joint plot of lexical correspondence analysis (frequencies are in parentheses)

4.2 Lexical Non Symmetrical Correspondence Analysis

Non Symmetrical Correspondence Analysis (NSCA) is proposed to study dependence in a contingency table. Instead of decomposing Pearson's ϕ^2, NSCA decomposes a predictability index, Goodman and Kruskal's τ_b:

$$\tau_b = \frac{\sum_{k-1}^{p} \sum_{j-1}^{V} \left[\left(f_{jk} - f_{j.} f_{k.} \right)^2 / f_k \right]}{1 - \sum_{j-1}^{V} f_{j.}^2} \tag{5}$$

In TDA, Lexical NSCA can be proposed to understand the dependence by vocabulary (open-ended questions) on document categories (closed questions). In general, we consider Lexical NSCA for exploring the linguistic behavior of respondents depending on some other characteristic(s). NSCA analyses the jth conditional distribution $f_{jk}/f_{.k}$ w.r.t. the independence hypothesis $f_{j.}$. In NSCA the distances between couples of category points are computed differently in the space spanned by the conditioning variable and the dependent variable. The distance between points that represent the categories of the explanatory variable is measured with a usual Euclidean metrics, while, in the other space, a weighted Euclidean metrics is adopted for standardising axes w.r.t. the marginal distribution as in CA. From an algebraic viewpoint, choosing NSCA means imposing different ortho-normalising constraints in the singular value decomposition of the profile matrix $\mathbf{FD_j^{-1}}$:

$$\mathbf{FD}_j^{-1} = \mathbf{U}'\Lambda\mathbf{V}' \tag{6}$$

$$\mathbf{U}'\mathbf{U} = \mathbf{V}'\mathbf{D}_j^{-1}\mathbf{V} = \mathbf{I} \tag{7}$$

The different ortho-normalising constraints on axes avoid the "zoom" effect, when there are infrequent categories (and this is often the case, dealing with words). The negative consequence is that it is impossible to draw joint plots, as the scale units on axes are completely different.

The main difference in reading the factorial planes produced by a NSCA consists in:

1. the dispersion of points around the origin shows how strong is the dependence of the linguistic behavior of respondents on the categorical variable(s) considered for grouping respondents (measured by τ_b)
2. if two words are closed, in the factorial plane they similarly depend on the categorical variable(s);
3. if two categories are close they similarly influence vocabulary;
4. joint plot has to be avoided;
5. the importance of a category is proportional to its distance from the origin.

By reading Fig. 3, we can see different marketing strategies. *Piemonte and Toscana* wines do not need to describe *essere, terra, vino*, while the other regions have to represent their characteristics unknown to consumers (*bianco, rosso, DOC*).

5 Conjoint Analysis with Textuals External Information

The strategy that will be described in the following has been proposed by Balbi et al. (2008) in designing new products and market segmentation. The interviewees were doubly asked for answering to the same question, first giving a free description of her/his ideal product and in a second step by choosing among a reduced number of categories. This proposal aims at overcoming the usual practice of referring to qualitative or to quantitative methods, alternatively.

Here we try to introduce some degrees of subjectivity in a quantitative approach. The multivariate statistical analysis typical for solving this problem is Conjoint Analysis (CoA) (Green and Srinivasan 1990). CoA aims at estimating the importance of a characteristic in the consumer preference structure. The estimate is computed for each individual. A questionnaire designed for performing CoA should have a section specifically planned for this aim, additionally to the classical sections asking for socio-demographic characteristics of the interviewee and other information usually related to his/her consumer behavior.

The most common way of collecting the preference structure is the so called "full profile" method, where alternatives of the same characteristics of the product are combined according to an experimental design matrix $\mathbf{X}(\mathbf{S}, L)$, partitioned in H juxtaposed indicator matrices $\mathbf{X}_h(h = 1, \ldots, H)$, where H is the number of

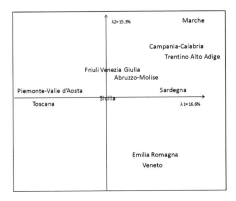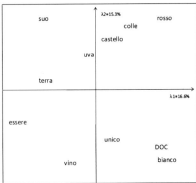

Fig. 3 Lexical non symmetrical correspondence analysis on Italian wines

characteristics considered for describing the S alternative products and L is the sum of the attributes for all the variables. The N interviewees are asked to give a rank or a score to the alternatives. Let $\mathbf{Y}(S, N)$ be the matrix having in column the score or rank given by the ith individual ($i = 1, \ldots, N$) to the S alternative products. The usual CoA model can be written as a multiple multivariate regression model (assuming to deal with measurements, although it is not often the case),

$$\mathbf{Y} = \mathbf{XB} + \mathbf{E} \tag{8}$$

where $\mathbf{E}(S, N)$ is the error matrix, which has in columns the errors of each individual model and $\mathbf{B}(L, N)$ is the matrix of the N individual part-worth coefficients associated to the L attribute levels; estimated by

$$\widehat{\mathbf{B}} = (\mathbf{X'X})^{-1}\mathbf{X'Y} \tag{9}$$

If $\mathbf{X'X}$ is singular, Moore-Penrose generalized inverse of $(\mathbf{X'X})^{-}$ may be computed. A multidimensional approach to CoA has been proposed in Lauro et al. (1998) in order to visualize part-worth coefficients in a low-dimensional space. A factorial decomposition of the matrix $(\mathbf{Y'X}(\mathbf{X'X})^{-}\mathbf{X'Y})$ has been proposed too. From a geometrical viewpoint the method consists in a principal component analysis performed on the images of the column vectors of the preference matrix $\mathbf{Y}$ on the disjoint subspaces spanned by the column vectors of the design matrix partitions $\mathbf{X}_h$. The geometrical approach to CoA was extended in Giordano and Scepi (1999) by introducing an additional matrix $\mathbf{Z}$, as external information on respondents' characteristics.

A crucial point in designing a CoA questionnaire is the choice of the characteristics and of their levels. In market research practice qualitative methods, first of all *focus groups*, are used for the preliminary identification of characteristics. This can be very expensive and it can induce misunderstanding in the descriptions of the ideal products. We propose the introduction of an open-ended question, positioned before the full profile alternatives, in order to obtain a description of the ideal product from respondents. We can consider textual information as external information. We introduce **T** for linearly constraining the **B** matrix, and we build the **Q** matrix of dimension (V, L):

$$Q = (TT')^- TB' = W \Xi V' \qquad (10)$$

whose general element is the estimated parameter linking the attribute levels to the individual textual descriptions of the ideal product. The SVD of the **Q** is performed. In this way, we can visualise the terms in the verbal descriptions together with the CoA levels on a common principal plane. The information about the respondents' characteristics can be projected as supplementary variables (Lebart et al. 1984), so to enrich global interpretation of CoA results.

5.1 The Watch Market

We illustrate our proposal with an application on the watch market. A sample of 150 individuals, stratified with respect to age and gender has been interviewed. The questionnaire consists of four section:

1. socio-demographic characteristics;
2. interest for watches (number of watches; interest on the brand; main reasons for choosing a watch)
3. the open question: "Describe your ideal watch"
4. alternatives watches, with respect to six binary variables: the *strap* (*steel or leather*), *mechanism* (*swiss or digital*), *winding up* (*manual or battery*), *model* (*classic or chrono*), *date* (*presence or absence*), *alarm* (*presence or absence*).

The design has been factorised in order to reduce the number of combinations.

In the analysis of the answers to the open-ended question, pre-processing have been performed and a vocabulary of 215 textual forms (partially grammatically marked) has been made out. Furthermore, a stop list was considered to eliminate the instrumental terms and a threshold was introduced for infrequent terms. Figure 4 shows the CoA levels on the first factorial plane (44 % of the total inertia). We can see a first segmentation of the market of an ideal watch: on the first factorial axis we have the opposition of consumers preferring traditional watches (right side of the map) versus consumers preferring modern ones (on the left side). Note that in the description of the different eventual watches the level "classic" is opposite to "chrono". If we add words on the map, we find that the repeated segment "classic model" and the word "classic" are on the left. This suggests the risk of a verbal misunderstanding so that marketing staff has to be careful in using, for example, the opposition classic/modern in a promotional campaign.

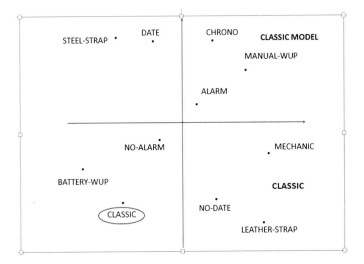

Fig. 4 Factorial representations of the market segmentation

6 Concluding Remarks

The answers given to open-ended questions in a survey are often discarded by researchers. The main reason is the difficulty of analysing them together with the answers given to closed-ended questions. The most common procedure consists in a manual post-coding, which is a difficult and expansive task. The alternative is given by automatically transforming the textual fragments in a structured data-base to be combined with the classical database consisting of answers to closed-ended questions. It is worth noting that this different approach does not consist in building new numerical variables, but in producing a peculiar data structure, mainly the lexical table. The principal consequence is a new challenging perspective, that of exploring and proposing new methods for the joint analysis of answers to closed and open-ended questions. In this paper we illustrated a famous technique proposed in literature with this aim, i.e. the LCA, with its non symmetrical version, and a method proposed for a peculiar situation: designing a new product in a Conjoint Analysis scheme, introducing textual external information. The new methods for analysing "non-traditional" data and the algorithmic developments related to Text Mining can contribute to develop this research field, together with attention to multinational surveys (Becue-Bertaut et al. 2010).

References

Balbi, S. (1995). Non symmetrical correspondence analysis of textual data and confidence regions for graphical forms. In S. Bolasco et al. (Eds.) *Actes des 3es Journées internationales d'Analyse statistique des Donnèes Textuelles*, (Vol. 2, pp. 5–12). Roma: CISU.

Balbi, S., Infante, G., & Misuraca, M. (2008). Conjoint analysis with textual external information. In S. Heiden et al. (Eds.) *JADT 2006*, (Vol. 1, pp. 129–136).

Becue-Bertaut, M., Fernandez-Aguirre, K., & Modrono-Herrán, J. I. (2010). Analysis of a mixture of closed and open-ended questions in the case of multilingual survey. *Advances in Data Analysis, Statistics for Industry and Technology, Part 1*, 21–31.

Benzecri, J. P. (1973). *L'Analyse des Correspondances*. Paris: Dunod.

Bolasco, S.: Statistica testuale e text mining: alcuni paradigmi applicativi. *Quaderni di Statistica, 7*, 17–53.

Giordano, G., & Scepi, G. (1999). Different informative structures for quality design. *Journal of Italian Statistical Society, 8*(2–3), 139–149.

Green, P. E., & Srinivasan, V. (1990). Conjoint analysis in marketing: new developments with implications for research and practice. *The Journal of Marketing, 54*(4), 3–19.

Lauro, C.N., Giordano, G., & Verde, R. (1998). A multidimensional approach to conjoint analysis. *Applied Stochastic Models and Data Analysis, 14*, 265–274.

Lebart, L., Morineau, A., & Warwick, K. (1984). *Multivariate descriptive statistical analysis*. New York: Wiley.

Lebart, L., Salem, A., & Berry, E. (1991). Recent developments in the statistical processing of textual data. *Applied Stochastic Models and Data Analysis, 7*, 47–62.

The Use of Self-Anchoring Scales in Social Research: The Cantril Scale for the Evaluation of Community Action Orientation

Immacolata Di Napoli and Caterina Arcidiacono

Abstract In this study we provide a thorough analysis of the properties of self-anchoring rating scales that give to respondents the chance to self-anchor according to their responses. In social sciences the reflexive perspective suggests that the researcher's opinions do not prevail over those of the respondents. Self-anchoring category rating scales seem to fulfill this requirement, since they allow respondents to define the anchor items by referring their personal experiences to the construct being measured. By way of example, we present a research on action in the participants' social contexts and the criteria defined for its description and measurement, which led to the use of a self-anchoring scale.

1 Introduction

Since the 20th century, social sciences have been investigating the meaning and applicability of measurements in the study of properties of social interactions which are not directly observable, such as attitudes, perceptions and opinions (Corbetta 1999).

As a matter of fact, the study of attitudes and opinions is one of the privileged areas of research of social psychology. The idea of evaluating, measuring, as well as of defining opinions and thoughts with the aim of creating a mutual system of priorities and hierarchies has long fascinated psychosocial scientists.

I. Di Napoli (✉) · C. Arcidiacono
Incoparde Laboratory, Department of Theories and Methods of Human and Social Sciences,
University of Naples Federico II, Napoli, Italy
e-mail: immacolata.dinapoli@unina.it

C. Arcidiacono
e-mail: caterina.arcidiacono@unina.it

C. Davino and L. Fabbris (eds.), *Survey Data Collection and Integration*,
DOI: 10.1007/978-3-642-21308-3_5, © Springer-Verlag Berlin Heidelberg 2013

The choice of a measuring scale involves two main stages: identifying the features of the objects to be measured and defining rules to associate numbers/symbols to the objects according to the characteristics of the scale.

We took, in fact a reflexive perspective, understood as the constant awareness and assessment of a researcher regarding his or her own contribution and influence on findings. In this case was it aimed at ensuring that the researcher's opinions do not prevail over those of the respondents, has also focused on avoiding the risk of incorrect or mistaken attributions of data due to the structure and characteristics of the research tools and/or to the researchers actions and decisions.

This approach brings to light the need to identify tools to define opinions and beliefs, the measuring parameter being in the hands of the respondent, thus inviting the researcher to re-define the criteria for quantifying and measuring the variables rather than act him or herself as their interpreter. In this paper we will present the theoretical and methodological choices made in constructing and defining a self-anchoring scale to measure the orientation of people towards taking part in projects to the benefit of their own local communities.

Therefore, we would like to report here some reflections concerning the importance of the action in the subjects' social contexts and the criteria defined for its description and measurement, which led to the use of a self-anchoring category rating scale.

2 Measuring Attitudes and Opinions

Following Stevens' methodological proposal (Stevens 1946), in social sciences there is no single measuring procedure but, because of the complexity of social reality, several procedures or measuring scales must be taken into consideration. The scale of measurement theory envisages several rules to assign numbers to the measured features, hence the existence of several scales of measurement (nominal, ordinal, interval and ratio scales) having peculiar mathematical properties and requiring the applicability of well-defined statistical procedures.

Marradi (1981) stresses the importance of reviewing the scaling techniques used in social research, based on the crucial distinction between continuous and discrete properties. In particular, Marradi (1981) criticizes the theory of scales defined by Stevens because of the stretching of the term "measurement", that is to say extending the idea of measurement to scales entailing counting alone, and/or arranging the features under study. In this sense, the Author suggests to redefine the concept of measurement. He points out that in social sciences there are objects with continuous features which, differently from natural sciences, do not have units of measurement since these are not defined a priori without the subject's collaboration.

Therefore, many of the properties relevant to social sciences, such as psychic properties, opinions, attitudes or values (authoritarianism, social cohesion, familism), can be conceived of as continuous, just like measurable continuous properties. However, unlike the latter, there is no unit of measurement for them, hence the need to use scaling techniques, which may produce variables untreatable as cardinal and variables treated as cardinal, depending on how the properties of measures are conceived of. What we wish to do here is to discuss and compare the qualities of the use of two scaling models defining ordinal and cardinal variables respectively: the Likert scale, acknowledged for and applied to the measurement of attitudes for years, and the self-anchoring scale put forward by Cantril (1965).

2.1 The Likert Scale

In 1932 the scale devised by Likert provided an answer which would satisfy applied research for long time. The Likert scale includes a number of items which can identify the underlying property we wish to measure; then a respondent must express the degree of his or her agreement on a certain "agree/disagree" gradient, where all the responses of a Likert scale are semantically labelled (strongly agree, agree, disagree, strongly disagree).

In the rating scale the subject adopts an absolute reference (Schifini D'Andrea 1999), whereby s/he classifies the object/stimulus in one of two or more classes a priori defined. Each subject evaluates by placing or associating the considered object/stimulus to the appropriate position, choosing from a series of positions defined beforehand. The researcher may give a score to each of the answers provided to each item and then consider summarizing the central tendency of responses by using either the median or the mode.

In this scale the distance between different categories cannot be quantified. The only possible operation is to determine whether a certain state is greater or smaller than another: the variables produced are, then, ordered categories. In this sense, the measured properties are considered to be continuous, while its states are viewed as discrete.

In-depth analyses on the quality of measurements, that the Likert scale provides, have highlighted some possible distortions which may be related to the respondent (acquiescence, desirability, response-set) or to the research tool (arbitrary distance between the categories, curvilinearity). Notwithstanding, we must admit that, despite its methodological limits, the Likert scale is widely used and is still considered a major instrument for social research.

2.2 Reflexivity and the Self-Anchoring Scale

The fundamental criterion to validate qualitative research (Mantovani 2010) today is the issue of reflexivity. Elsewhere we have emphasized the importance for the researcher to be "on the field", and reflexivity was put forward as his or her specific object of education and investigation (Arcidiacono 2009).

We agree with Kaneklin (2008, 2010) that the true resource of research is inter-subjectivity: in doing research, rationality is connected to sensoriality and relationality and, in these terms, the researcher's scientific involvement cannot be only intellectual.

These needs are emphasised in qualitative research methodologies, but how can we take them into account also in a quantitative approach that has the ambition to achieve the measurement of the phenomena investigated?

While agreeing on the importance and central role of the intersubjective dimension in the research process, we believe it is essential to consider and identify the filling out of a self-report questionnaire as the context and expression of inter-subjectivity in a mainly quantitative research approach and provide a full answer to this question in the self-anchoring category rating scale.

The self-anchoring scale was developed by Kilpatrick and Cantril as an attempt to apply the first-person approach to the measurement of psychological variables. The position held by the transactional theory is that the world of reality is always unique up to a certain degree since everyone has unique past experiences and purposes (Kilpatrick and Cantril 1960).

The characteristic of this group of techniques consists, in fact, in its considering the subjects as being capable of assessing their own status regarding the specific quality or property identified. For this reason these scaling techniques are also known as self-anchoring, self-rating or autographic scales.

With self-anchoring scales, the respondent himself or herself (in the case of a sufficiently self-aware individual) evaluates his or her status regarding the specific quality or property under consideration and expresses it by means of a process of spatial or numerical representation that can be very far from his or her usual operations in daily life (Marradi 1996).

When using the self-anchoring scale, the respondent is asked to assess cognitive objects as individuals, groups, institutions, events listed by individual words or expressions and, before deciding on his or her position, s/he is instructed to identify the two extremes as the worst and the best possible.

In self-anchoring scales each respondent provides an individual definition of the end points of a dimension and then rates him or herself on this self-defined continuum. Specifically, for each answer, individuals can express their degree of agreement upon a line 10 cm long, which is then calculated in a fixed range (from 1 to 10).

The hypothesis is that, by positioning him-/herself, the individual interprets the length of the intervals and also the unit of measurement so that there is an equal subdivision of the single dimensions (Corbetta 1999). The advantage of the self-anchoring scale is that it does not provide an intermediate alternative corresponding to a specific characteristic. In this way the respondents are not induced to assume a "medium position" and are helped to take sides with their answers.

The assessment is encoded by means of a process of numerical representation and, after encoding, it is possible to treat the variables as cardinal. Self-anchoring scales thus generate "almost cardinal" variables because they represent properties that are not effectively measurable, but are treated in all respects as cardinal (Amaturo 2009).

With self-anchoring scales the unit of measurement is not established by the researcher (R), but by the interviewees (I), who place themselves on a hypothetical continuum. In these cases it is therefore necessary to have the active cooperation of respondents, who evaluate their status concerning each specific quality or property.

In the following we point out some specific features of the Cantril scale that constitute its advantages and peculiarity in comparison with Likert scale:

1. It does not transform a categorical assessment into a numerical value (see the score that someone assigns with the Likert scale): it allows subjects to express a personal assessment directly by a numerical value that can be measured and compared.
2. Self-anchoring scales could be valuable for cross-cultural comparison (Cantril 1965; Bernheim et al. 2006). In fact, research has shown that Likert scales with fixed anchors suffer from some cultural biases (Chen et al. 1995; Lee et al. 2002), while self-anchoring scales are able to resolve this cultural bias as they explicitly take the respondent's frame of reference into account when asking to compare a given situation with the respondent's personal situation (Bloom et al. 1999).
3. Within a constructionist and reflexive perspective, strength lies in the expression of the interviewee's assessment rather than an evaluation system determined by the researcher, who does not therefore assign an "arbitrary" number (score) to an ordinal categorisation.

The Cantril scale is therefore a scale that provides almost cardinal variables. The Likert scale, instead, involves ordinal variables, since only the order of the response is guaranteed, while the distance between them is entirely unknown.

The latter is very popular in psychosocial research, where the researcher is required to assign a numerical score to a qualitative assessment (strongly agree, agree, uncertain, disagree, strongly disagree), and very few authors (Corbetta 1999) prefer self-anchoring scales. We must bear in mind, however, that the latter is quasi-cardinal, because we are not sure that each level's interpretation is shared by all involved subjects.

Hofmans et al. (2009) found out that a self-anchoring scale seems to be psychometrically equivalent to a rating scale with fixed anchors, and pointed out that a self-anchoring scale should be the preferred choice when a researcher wishes to obtain additional qualitative information, while rating scales with fixed anchors are preferable to self-anchoring rating scales when the group of research participants is homogeneous, in order to avoid increased workload and dropout.

This disparity in the frequency of use of the Likert and self anchoring scales is even more evident in a comparative examination of the following terms in Google Scholar (English version): by typing "Likert scale", we found 173,000 references in the English version of Google Scholar and 1,460 in the Italian version; "Semantic differential" has 332,000 references (Google Italian version: 3,640); "Cantril scale" 1,290 references (It. 100); "Emotion thermometer" 25,900 references; "Forced Choice scale" 1,730,000 references (quotations in It. pages 1,250).

Marradi and Gasperoni (2002) carefully examined how the Likert scale (the method of summated ratings of 1932) is used, in the most varied circumstances (in relation to the semantic differential, the forced choice, etc.), but not in relation to the Cantril scale. In the literature we find that the Cantril Self-Anchoring Striving Scale (Cantril 1965) has been used since the 1960s and is a favourite of Daniel Kahneman's. The Gallup (2011) describes the following application of the technique:

> Please imagine a ladder with steps numbered from zero at the bottom to 10 at the top.
> The top of the ladder represents the best possible life for you and the bottom of the ladder represents the worst possible life for you.
> On which step of the ladder would you say you personally feel you stand at this time? (ladder-present)
> On which step do you think you will stand about five years from now? (ladder-future)

An adaptation of Cantril's methodology, used to study quality of life, is the Self-Anchoring Self-Esteem Scale (SASES). Further use is in the study of life satisfaction measured by the response to the so-called Cantril scale. This measures life satisfaction on a 0–10 scale, like steps on the so-called ladder of life. This measure of life satisfaction is also referred to in the literature as the Self-Anchoring Striving Scale (SASS).

The Cantril scale has been shown to have adequate reliability and validity (Beckie and Hayduk 2007; McIntosh 2001). According to Diener et al. (1999), when self-reports of wellbeing are correlated with other methods of measurement, they show an adequate convergent validity. Although it is impossible to determine whether a value (score) has the same meaning for all respondents, this internal criterion of differences can however be eliminated by using the technique of deflation (removing the effect of the subject using only a part of the scale). The same procedure can also help avoiding systematic biases, specifically when self-anchoring scales provide a large number of modes of response (particularly the feeling thermometer using a 1–100 scale) which can lead to always use the same range, e.g. intermediate or high scores.

We used the Cantril scale in different research works: as an evaluation scale of user satisfaction for women attending a course on parenting skills with the objective to assess parents' satisfaction and interest (Arcidiacono 2007); as an assessment tool of specific skills acquired, and level of competence of teachers in a course aimed at teachers and social workers regarding the organisation of courses on the theme of peace.

In Sect. 3 we will give a specific explanation concerning the reasons that led us to build and develop a Cantril scale aimed at measuring a new construct of community psychology: community action orientation.

3 The Construction of a Self–Anchoring Scale for Community Action Orientation

3.1 Preliminary Steps

The literature in community psychology presents various constructs—attachment to place and sense of place (Proshansky et al. 1983), community identity (Puddifoot 1995; Lalli 1992)—and proposes several instruments of measurement. These concepts have in common the dimension of belonging as their central element.

The model of sense of community (McMillan and Chavis 1986) best explains the interconnections between people and their environments and describes the way in which members of a community feel that they belong to it, that they are important for others and that they have been nurtured in trust to satisfy each other's needs.

Arcidiacono et al. (2012) explored in depth how the sense of community is considered to be the key indicator correlated with the perception of inclusion in the community one belongs to (Mashek et al. 2007) as well as one's social wellbeing, with perceived support (Dalton et al. 2001; Herrero and Gracia 2007; Pretty 1990) and with social participation (Davidson et al. 1991; Tartaglia 2006).

Brodsky et al. (Brodksy 2006; Brodksy et al. 1999; Brodksy and Marx 2001) emphasize that this indicator should be seen as the meaning and significance that the community takes on for the individual in terms of qualities, values and costs, both in a positive and in a negative way.

Chavis (2006) highlights the central role of the sense of belonging among citizens who carry out local community projects. Nevertheless, other studies conducted in the south of Italy (Arcidiacono 2004; Arcidiacono and Procentese 2005; Arcidiacono et al. 2007; Arcidiacono and Di Napoli 2008a,b) have indicated that neither the sense of belonging nor the sense of community provide reliable clues regarding how the individual will act in the community at the personal, relational and community levels (Prilleltensky and Nelson 2002).

These studies suggest that the sense of belonging to a community does not have a transformative power to promote social action: so, as the central aspect for orientation to project action, Arcidiacono (2004) proposed the dimension of trust meant as an expectancy value towards territorial community, in which two main factors can be identified: usefulness and the value attributed to its consequences.

Then we constructed a specific and adequate scale, according to the Cantril approach, to collect information about the orientation to act in the community.

3.2 Identifying Indicators of Community Action Orientation

In the dialogic perspective, the interactive exchange between two interlocutors is the outcome of a joint activity of meaning production, where possible misunderstandings are an excellent spur to activate dialogue between the multiple cultures of each of the interlocutors (Habermans 1981; Procentese and Di Napoli 2010) and to modify the researcher's cultural symbolic system (Mantovani 1995). The construct of interactive universalism, which Benhabib (2006) introduced as the meta level of dialogue analysis transcending the 'here and now' interaction, makes it possible to reach a relational dimension, as an opportunity to build new forms of social bonds (Galimberti 1994; Gumperz 1982).

In this perspective, the identification of indicators constitutes one of the crucial stages in the construction of an instrument of investigation. It is paramount to hold an in-depth knowledge of the existing literature on the topic, whereby the researcher identifies the conceptual dimensions to be measured and operationalises them, responding to criteria of clarity, homogeneity and unambiguous language. In order to remain within the framework of a reflexive (Schön 1983) and dialogic approach, we considered it appropriate to rest our work on the direct involvement of the people for whom the tool has been designed even when constructing the indicators for the scale of measurement concerning people's orientation to act in the community.

We held focus groups with young students, with whom we discussed and defined a first set of items. The process to give these items a new meaning, which we carried out with the protagonists, enriched with further dimensions and peculiar aspects the positive expectations these young citizens had toward the local context they belonged to, thus extending the instrument to other items which had not been included before (Arcidiacono et al. 2007).

Here, in a reflexive dialogic perspective, we highlight that the construction of an instrument is the outcome of a constant process of exchange between the researcher's and the respondent's conceptual universes.

Hence the need to choose a model of measurement which responded mainly to the need to preserve a dialogic approach during the administration of the instrument, more specifically to the respondent's answering mode.

3.3 The Community Action Orientation Scale

Research on the Community Action Orientation scale (CAO) is an example of the application of the self-anchoring scale, of which we report some of the main statistical results produced with the aim of analysing the dialogic and reflexive value of the administration procedure.

CAO is a new concept in community psychology. According to (Bloom et al. 1999), self-anchoring scales are most useful to validate constructs which have not been theorised.

In our case this concept concerns the expectations and orientations of people about being socially active in their local community.

The scale we first constructed consisted of 37 items: 21 items related to the present and 16 specifically directed to the future (Arcidiacono and Di Napoli 2008a).

This instrument, filled out by a sample of 686 youth aged 18–35 (Arcidiacono and Di Napoli 2008a), has been compared with other instruments: the Scale of Social

Wellbeing (an indicator of the quality of relations with others and with the extended social context) and the Scale of Community Identity Questionnaire (an indicator of the affective and cognitive dimensions of the bonds with one's community). The comparison of these tools, by means of correlation and factorial analyses, has shown a poor relationship between orientation towards community identity and Social Well-Being (Keyes 1998) [Italian version (Cicognani and Albanesi 2001)], as well as an opposite one between Community Orientation Action and Community Response Questionnaire (Arcidiacono et al. 2007).

However, the need for a more specific focus of the instrument led us to choose only the set of items related to the present (21) and select the manifest variables of community action orientation in order to explore and reveal its latent variables. In this further study, only the present perspective was taken into account, whereas the items (17;18;19;20) related to the expectations for the community's future were excluded. The CAO items related to the present referred to the respondent's expectations in relation to the status quo of his/her current community:

(i)   four items referred to the evaluation of public administration and the opportunities offered by the local community;
(ii) five items related to the relationships established by the individual with his/her fellow citizens, and to how the citizens were involved in their local community;
(iii) eight items were designed to reveal the individuals willingness to take part in different initiatives and to realise their own life plans in the community.

Each answer was given a score according to a structured self-anchoring scale. For each answer, respondents expressed the degree of their agreement by putting a cross upon a line 10 cm in length. After an exploratory factorial analysis using principal component analysis and replicability of the factorial solution, we identified a final, simpler version made up of 14 items, organised into three latent variables: Competence and efficacy of the territorial community; Expectations of personal, collective and contextual potentialities; Territorial community as a chosen place for personal pleasure.

To evaluate the reliability of the scale we propose the Cronbach's alfa coefficient. In similar contexts the threshold coefficient is fixed at 0.6 (Cronbach and Shavelson 2004) and for all the three factors we obtain an α value greater then this.

The instrument's administration procedure is a further step with a view to avoiding dropouts, which, according to Hofmans et al. (2009), might be related to an excessive workload on the respondents.

Emphasizing a dialogic approach, our administration procedure always included the following steps:

(a) the researcher briefly introduces the research topic;
(b) the researcher invites participants to express their reflections on the topic both in group and individual administrations;
(c) the researcher describes and illustrates the use of the anchoring scale;
(d) the self-report tool is administered in the presence of the researcher;

(e) on collection of the completed questionnaires, additional reflections can be gathered from the participants on both the topic and the use of the measuring scale.

All these steps enabled the researcher and participants to co-construct, dialogically, a frame of meaning in which the use of the scale took on a shared value. This contributed to guaranteeing respect for the selected interlocutors' subjectivities and avoiding dropout. While it can appear time- and energy-consuming for the researcher, a careful administration is the necessary precondition for the participant to take active part in the research proposed.

4 Final Considerations

By using the Cantril scale we defined items allowing the respondent to provide an answer to each question which fully responds to his/her point of view.

The scientific debate between the nomothetic and idiographic views which, according to Amerio (2000), has only apparently been overcome, found in the Cantril scale an instrument whereby it is possible to collect the uniqueness of data as well as to extend it to a larger population.

This intent, however, found an application in the gathering of data which can be operationalised at the statistical level of the Cantril scale, which differs from the better-known Likert scale in its scientific approach.

In the framework of a topical debate in social sciences on the researcher's role in defining the respondents' answers, we may agree with Amaturo (2009) that the Cantril scale makes it possible to gather the respondent's positioning rather than the researcher's interpretation of the respondent's point of view.

In this respect, in a reflexive, participatory perspective, a Cantril scale avoids biases caused by the researcher's interpretation and guarantees faithfulness to the respondent's positioning. This way the rigour of the data analysis combines with the awareness that the respondents were able to both express their point of view and position themselves in relation to the entirety of the issues investigated.

From the importance of reflexivity and subjectivity derived the need to describe the various stages in the research process and the need not to see this stage as secondary, but rather as participating in the construction of the scientific act.

It is a fact, after all, that outside the field of research, in consultancy recourse is widely made to solution-focused scaling questions which seem very similar to the self-anchoring scale and which have developed in a similar way over the years but do have some additional elements compared to the Cantril self-anchoring scale.

De Shazer (1985) began to investigate the idea of using numbers to describe one's feelings and life-situation. This led to the development of the scaling question used in solution-focused therapy (Malinen 2001). Today scaling questions have developed into the most well-known and frequently used solution-focused techniques. Scaling questions are relatively easy to use and extremely versatile. Nowadays, many therapists, coaches and managers use them, and even many people who know little about the solution-focused approach are familiar with scaling questions. Scientific research is left with the task to assess how this instrument can respond to the heuristic purposes of psycho-social sciences.

References

Amaturo, E. (2009). *Metodologia e tecnica della ricerca sociale*. http://www.federica.unina.it/corsi/metodologia-e-tecnica-della-ricerca-sociale Accessed 3 June 2011.

Amerio, P. (2000). Ottica nomotetica e ottica idiografica in psicologia sociale. *Rassegna di Psicologia, 3*, 129–145.

Arcidiacono, C. (2004). Sentiemento de comunidad y esperanza. In A. Sanchez Vidal, A. Palacín, & L. M. Constanzo Zambrano (Eds.) , *Psicologia Comunitaria Europea: Comunidad, Poder, Ètica y valores* (pp. 218–228). Barcelona: UB.

Arcidiacono, C. (2007). Prefazione. In M. Giordano, D. Artiaco, & N. Gasperini (a cura di) *Il villaggio, Buone Pratiche di Sostegno alla Genitorialità: Integrazioni di Percorsi di Vita, di Saperi, di Relazioni. Quaderni Fondazione Zoli* (pp. 5–8). Napoli: Pisanti Editore.

Arcidiacono, C. (2009). Riflessività, processualità, situatività: parole chiave della ricerca-azione. *Ricerche di psicologia*, numero speciale a cura di Colucci, F.P. *XXXII*, 113–126.

Arcidiacono, C., & Di Napoli, I. (2008a). Community trust: The Scale of Community Action Orientation (CAO). *Proceedings of the 7th International Conference on Social Science Methodology*. Naples, 1–5 September, 2008a. http://www.rc332008.unina.it/

Arcidiacono, C., & Di Napoli, I. (2008b) Sense of community: Agency versus sense of belonging. In C. Vázquez Rivera, M. Figuero Rodrìguez, W. Pacheco Bopu, & D. Pérez Jiménez (Eds.), *Psicologìa Comunitaria Internacional: Agendas Compartidas en la Diversidad*(pp. 259–284). Puerto Rico: Ed. UPR.

Arcidiacono, C., Di Napoli, I., & Sarnacchiaro, P. (2007). Puddifoot community identity and juvenile community action orientation. In A. Bokszczanin (Ed.), *Social Change in Solidarity: Community Psychology Perspectives and Approaches* (pp. 93–108). Opole: Opole University Press.

Arcidiacono, C., Di Napoli, I., Zampatti, E., & Procentese, F. (2012). Sense of community and orientation towards community in the campania region. In J. Ornelas, M. Vargaz (Eds.), *Building Participative Empowering and Diverse Communities*. Lisboa: Sociedade Portuguesa de Psicologia Comunitàri.

Arcidiacono, C., & Procentese, F. (2005). Distinctiveness and sense of community in the historical center of Naples: a piece of participatory action-research. *Journal of Community Psychology, 33*, 1–8.

Arcidiacono, C., Procentese, F., & Di Napoli, I. (2007) Youth, community belonging, planning and power. *Journal of Applied Social Psychology, 17*, 1–16.

Beckie, T. M., & Hayduk, L. A. (1997). Measuring quality of life. *Social Indicators Research, 42*, 21–39.

Benhabib, S. (2006). *I diritti degli altri. Stranieri, residenti, cittadini*. Milano: Raffaello Cortina Editore.

Bernheim, J. L., Theuns, P., Mazaheri, M., Hofmans, J., Fliege, H., & Rose, M. (2006). The potential of Anamnestic Comparative Self-Assessment (ACSA) to reduce bias in the measurement of subjective well-being. *Journal of Happiness Studies, 7*, 227–250

Bloom, M., Fischer, J., & Orme, J. (1999). *Evaluating practice: Guidelines for the accountable professional*(2nd ed.). Boston: Allyn & Bacon.

Brodsky, A. E. (1996). Resilient single mothers in risky neighborhoods: Negative psychological sense of community. *Journal of Community Psychology, 24*, 347–363.

Brodksy, A., & Marx, C. (2001). Layers of identity: Multiple psychological senses of community within a community setting. *Journal of Community Psychology, 29*, 161–178.

Brodsky, A., O'Campo, P., & Aronson, R. (1999). PSOC in community context: Multilevel correlates of a measure of psychological sense of community in low income, urban neighbourhoods. *Journal of Community Psychology, 27,* 659–679.

Cantril, H. (1965). *The Pattern of Human Concerns.* New Brunswick, NJ: Rutgers University Press.

Chavis, D. (2006). *Sense of community theory as a framework for community development strategies.* Paper presented at first international conference on community psychology, San Juan, Puerto Rico.

Chen, C., Lee, S. Y., & Stevenson, H. W. (1995). Response style and cross-cultural comparisons of rating scales among East Asian and North American students. *Psychological Science 6,* 170–175.

Cicognani, E., & Albanesi, C. (2001). Dimensioni del benessere sociale: applicazione di uno strumento di misurazione. *Psicologia della salute, 1,* 105–122.

Corbetta, P. (1999). *Metodologia e Tecniche della Ricerca Sociale.* Bologna: Il Mulino

Cronbach, L. J., Shavelson, R. J. (2004). My current thoughts on coefficient alpha and successor procedures. *Educational and Psychological Measurement, 64*(3), 391–418.

Dalton, J., Elias, M., & Wandersman, A. (2001). *Community psychology: Linking Individuals and Communities.* Stamford, CT: Wadsworth.

Davidson, W., Cotter, P., & Stovall, J. (1991). Social predispositions for the development of sense of community. *Psychological Reports, 68,* 817–818.

De Shazer, S. (1985). *Keys to Solution in Brief Therapy.* New York: Norton.

Diener, E., Suh, E. M., Lucas, R. E., & Smith, H. L. (1999). Subjective well-being: Three decades of progress. *Psychological Bulletin, 125,* 276–302.

Di Napoli, I., Arcidiacono, C., & Palumbo, F. (2011). How to measure community action orientation (submitted 2011).

Galimberti, C. (1994). Dalla comunicazione alla conversazione. *Ricerche di Psicologia, 18,* 113–152.

Gallup (2011). *Understanding How Gallup Uses the Cantril Scale.* http://www.gallup.com/poll/122453/understanding-gallup-uses-cantril-scale.aspx. Accessed 4 June 2011.

Gumperz, J.J. (1982). *Discourse strategies. Studies in interactional sociolinguistics* (Vol.1). Cambridge: Cambridge University Press.

Habermans, J. (1981) *Teorie des Kommunicativen.* Frankfurt am Main, Suhrkamp. (Trad. It. *La Teoria dell'Agire Comunicativo.* Il Mulino, Bologna, 1986).

Herrero, J., & Gracia, E. (2007). Measuring perceived community support: Factorial structure, longitudinal invariance, and predictive validity of the Perceived Community Support Questionnaire (PCSQ). *Journal of Community Psychology, 35,* 197–217.

Hofmans, J., Theuns, P., & Van Acker, F. (2009). Combining quality and quantity. A psychometric evaluation of the self-anchoring scale. *Quality & Quantity, 43,* 703–716.

Kaneklin, C. (2008). Elementi e requisiti della ricerca-azione. *Rivista di Psicologia di comunità, 2,* 39–41.

Kaneklin, C. (2010). *Il Gruppo in Teoria e in Pratica. L'Intersoggettività come Forza Produttiva.* Milano: Raffaello Cortina.

Keyes, C. L. M. (1998). Social well-being. *Social Psychological Quarterly, 61,* 121–140.

Kilpatrick, F. P., & Cantril, H. (1960). Self-anchoring scaling: A measure of individuals' unique reality worlds. *Journal of Individual Psychology, 16,* 158–173.

Lalli, M. (1992). Urban related identity: Theory, measurement and empirical findings. *Journal of Environmental Psychology, 12,* 285–303.

Lee, J. W., Jones, P. S., Mineyama, Y., & Zhang, X. E. (2002). Cultural differences in responses to a Likert scale. *Research in Nursing & Health, 25,* 295–306.

Likert, R. (1932). A technique for the measurement of attitudes. *Archives of Psychology, 140,* 5–55.

Malinen, T. (2001). In the whirl of the flowing river discussion with Elam Nunnally. (Virtaavan joen pyörteissä keskustelu Elam Nunnally kanssa). *Ratkes, 1,* 20–24.

Mantovani, G. (1995). *Comunicazione e identità.* Bologna: Il Mulino.

Mantovani, G. (2010). Fare ricerca "con", non "sugli" altri. Ma chi sono gli altri? In C. Arcidiacono, & F. Tuccillo, (Eds.), *Ricerca Interculturale e Processi di Cambiamento. Metodologie, Risorse e Aree Critiche.* Caserta: La Melagrana.

Marradi, A. (1981). Misurazione e scale: qualche riflessione e una proposta. *Quaderni di Sociologia, XXIX*, 595–639.

Marradi, A. (1996). Una lunga ricerca sui valori, e alcuni suoi strumenti. In A. Marradi, G. P. Prandstraller (Eds.), *L'etica dei Ceti Emergenti*. Milano: Franco Angeli.

Marradi, A., & Gasperoni, G. (2002). *Costruire il Dato 3 Le Scale Likert*. Milano: Franco Angeli.

Mashek, D., Cannaday, L. W., Tangney, J. P. (2007). Inclusion of community in self scale: A single-item pictorial measure of community connectedness. *Journal of Community Psychology, 35*, 257–275.

McIntosh, C. N. (2001). Report on the construct validity of the temporal satisfaction with life scale. *Social Indicators Research, 54*, 37–56.

McMillan, D., & Chavis, D. (1986). Sense of community: A definition and theory. *Journal of Community Psychology, 1*, 6–23.

Pretty, G. (1990). Relating psychological sense of community to social climate characteristics. *Journal of Community Psychology, 18*, 60–65.

Prilleltensky, I., & Nelson, G. (2002). *Doing psychology critically. Making a difference in diverse settings*. NewYork: Palgrave.

Procentese, F., & Di Napoli, I. (2010). L'incontro con l'altro nell'attuale contesto socio-culturale: quale sguardo nel lavoro del ricercatore? In C. Arcidiacono, F. Tuccillo (Eds.), *Ricerca Interculturale e Processi di Cambiamento*. La Melagrana, Caserta: Metodologie, Risorse e Aree Critiche.

Proshansky, H. N., Fabian, A., & Kaminoff, R. (1983). Place identity: Physical world and socialization of the self. *Journal of Environmental Psychology, 3*, 57–83.

Puddifoot, J. E. (1995). Dimensions of community identity. *Journal of Community and Applied Social Psychology, 5*, 357–370.

Schifini D'Andrea, S. (1999). La qualitá della vita: misure, teorie e modelli. In E. Aureli, F. Buratto, L. Carli Sardi, A. Franci, A. Ponti Sgargi, & S. Schifini D'Andrea (Eds.), *Contesti di Qualitá di Vita* (pp. 15–66). Milano: Franco Angeli.

Schön, D. A. (1983). The reflective practitioner: How professionals think in action. New York: Basic Books (trad. it. Schön, D.A.:Il professionista riflessivo. Per una nuova epistemologia della pratica, Dedalo, Bari, 1993).

Stevens, S. S. (1946). On the theory of scales of measurement. *Science, 103*, 677–680.

Tartaglia, S. (2006). A preliminary study for a new model of sense of community. *Journal of Community Psychology, 34*, 25–36.

Part III
Sampling Design and Error Estimation

Small Area Estimation of Poverty Indicators

Monica Pratesi, Caterina Giusti and Stefano Marchetti

Abstract The estimation of poverty, inequality and life condition indicators all over the European Union has become one topic of primary interest. A very common target is the core set of indicators on poverty and social exclusion agreed by the Laeken European Council in December 2001 and called Laeken indicators. They include measures of the incidence of poverty, such as the Head Count Ratio (also known as at-risk-of-poverty-rate) and of the intensity of poverty, as the Poverty Gap. Unfortunately, these indicators cannot be directly estimated from EU-SILC survey data when the objective is to investigate poverty at sub-regional level. As local sample sizes are small, the estimation must be done using the small area estimation approach. Limits and potentialities of the estimators of Laeken indicators obtained under EBLUP and M-quantile small area estimation approaches are discussed here, as well as their application to EU-SILC Italian data. The case study is limited to the estimation of poverty indicators for the Tuscany region. However, additional results are available and downloadable from the web site of the SAMPLE project, funded under the 7FP (http://www.sample-project.eu).

1 Introduction

In recent years, the estimation and dissemination of poverty, inequality and life condition indicators all over the European Union has become one topic of primary interest. Indeed, policy makers should establish their decisions on detailed information, and

M. Pratesi (✉) · C. Giusti · S. Marchetti
Department of Statistics and Mathematics Applied to Economics, University of Pisa (Italy),
Pisa, Italy
e-mail: m.pratesi@ec.unipi.it

C. Giusti
e-mail: caterina.giusti@ec.unipi.it

S. Marchetti
e-mail: stefano.marchetti@ec.unipi.it

C. Davino and L. Fabbris (eds.), *Survey Data Collection and Integration*,
DOI: 10.1007/978-3-642-21308-3_6, © Springer-Verlag Berlin Heidelberg 2013

this information should be referred to appropriate domains. This is particularly true in Italy, a country characterized by large variability in terms of living conditions between regions and provinces; this variability is often comparable to that of the EU as a whole (Brandolini and Saraceno 2007).

So far poverty maps have become a very powerful tool for targeting mechanisms to design better policies and interventions. This renewed attention extends beyond the academic community with National Statistical Offices around the world showing interest in poverty estimation methodologies. This interest is also reflected in the major investment that the European Commission has made by funding the research project Small Area Methods for Poverty and Living condition Estimates (SAMPLE—http://www.sample-project.eu) and the research project Advanced Methodology for European Laeken Indicators (AMELI—http://www.uni-trier.de).

Until very recently the practice of poverty mapping has been driven by the World Bank method proposed by Elbers et al. (2003). It combines individual/household survey data and population data with the objective of estimating poverty indicators for specific geographic areas as small as villages or hamlets. More recently, researchers in the small area estimation field have intensively studied the World Bank method and have proposed small area models for poverty mapping. Two such recent methods are the M-quantile approach (Chambers and Tzavidis 2006; Tzavidis et al. 2010) and the Empirical Best Prediction (EBP) approach proposed by Molina and Rao (2010).

In this paper we will focus on limits and potentialities of the estimators obtained under these approaches and describe the results of their application to European Union-Statistics on Income and Living Conditions (EU-SILC) Italian data. Our objective is the construction of poverty maps of Laeken poverty indicators for those areas or domains where the use of direct estimators doesn't allow reliable estimates. The case study is limited here to the poverty indicators for the Tuscany region. Additional results are available and downloadable from the SAMPLE project web site (http://www.sample-project.eu).

2 Poverty Indicators

Among poverty indicators the so called Laeken indicators are used to target poverty and inequalities for comparisons between countries. They are a core set of statistical indicators on poverty and social exclusion agreed by the European Council in December 2001, in the Brussels suburb of Laeken, Belgium. They include measures of the incidence of poverty, such as the Head Count Ratio (also known as at-risk-of-poverty-rate) and of the intensity of poverty, such as the Poverty Gap.

In many cases these measures are considered as a starting point for more in depth studies of poverty and living conditions. In fact, analyses are done using also non-monetary indicators in order to give a more complete picture of poverty and deprivation (Cheli and Lemmi 1995). As poverty is a question of graduation, the set of indicators is generally enlarged with other indicators of belonging to vulnerable

groups from which it can be likely to enter into the status of poverty (for details, see
SAMPLE project results).

Laeken indicators are computed every year on a comparable basis in each EU
country using data coming from official sample surveys such as the EU-SILC
survey. They are estimated using the so called direct estimators based on regression estimation and calibration theory (for Italy see ISTAT 2008).

However, due to the cost constraints in the design of the major official surveys,
the EU-SILC survey is designed to obtain reliable estimates only at regional level
(NUTS-2 level).[1] Thus, in order to satisfy the increasing demand from official and
private institutions of statistical estimates on poverty and living conditions referring
to smaller unplanned domains (that is provinces and municipalities), there is the need
to resort to small area methodologies.

Here we focus exclusively on the estimation of two Laeken poverty indicators,
the incidence of poverty or *Head Count Ratio* (HCR) and the *Poverty Gap* (PG), as
denoted in the generalized measures of poverty introduced by Foster et al. (1984).
Denoting by t the poverty line, the Foster, Greer and Thorbecke (FGT) poverty
measures for a small area d are defined as:

$$F_{\alpha d} = \frac{1}{N_d} \sum_{j=1}^{N_d} \left(\frac{t - y_{jd}}{t}\right)^{\alpha} \mathrm{I}(y_{jd} \leq t). \qquad (1)$$

The poverty line t is a level of income that defines the state of poverty (units
with income below t are considered poor), y is a measure of income for individ-
ual/household j, N_d is the number of individuals/households in area d, I is the
indicator function (equal to 1 when $y_{jd} \leq t$ and 0 otherwise) and α is a "sensitivity"
parameter. When $\alpha = 0$, $F_{\alpha d}$ is the *Head Count Ratio* whereas when $\alpha = 1$, $F_{\alpha d}$ is
the *Poverty Gap*.

The HCR indicator is a widely used measure of poverty. The popularity of this
indicator is due to its ease of construction and interpretation. At the same time this
indicator also assumes that all poor household/individuals are in the same situation.
For example, the easiest way of reducing the headcount index is by targeting benefits
to people just below the poverty line because they are the ones who are cheapest to
move across the line. Hence, policies based on the headcount index might be sub-
optimal. For this reason we also obtain estimates of the PG indicator. The PG can be
interpreted as the average shortfall of poor people. It shows how much would have
to be transferred to the poor to bring their expenditure up to the poverty line.

In this paper we calculate the HCR and the PG referring to households as statistical
units, and to household equivalised disposable income as a measure of income. The
household equivalised disposable income is calculated as the household total net
income divided by the equivalised household size according to Eurostat (2007),
which gives a weight of 1.0 to the first adult, 0.5 to other persons aged 14 or over

---

[1] The Nomenclature of Territorial Units for Statistics is a procedure standard by Eurostat for
referencing the subdivision of countries for statistical purposes.

who are living in the household and 0.3 to each child aged less than 14. In addition to the HCR and PG we also calculate the mean of the household equivalised income in the areas of interest. As an alternative, the same indicators can be computed referring to the individuals as elementary statistical units (ISTAT 2010, p. 224).

In the next section we present the estimators that can be used to compute poverty indicators at the small area level.

3 Small Area Methods for the Estimation of Poverty Indicators

The straightforward approach to calculate FGT poverty indicators referring to the areas of interest is to compute direct estimates. For each area, direct estimators use only the data referring to the sampled households, since for these households the information on the household income is available. Let w_{jd} be the sampling weight (inverse of the probability of inclusion) of household j belonging to the n_d sampled observations from small area d, s_d.

The direct estimators of the FGT poverty indicators are of the form

$$F_{\alpha d}^{dir} = \frac{1}{\sum_{j \in s_d} w_{jd}} \sum_{j \in s_d} w_{jd} \left(\frac{t - y_{jd}}{t}\right)^\alpha I(y_{jd} < t), \quad d = 1, \ldots, D \quad \alpha = 0, 1,$$

(2)

where $\sum_{i \in s_d} w_{jd} = N_d$, the population size of small area d. In the same way, the mean of the household equivalised income in each small area can be computed as

$$m_d^{dir} = \frac{1}{\sum_{i \in s_d} w_{jd}} \sum_{j \in s_d} w_{jd} y_{jd}, \quad d = 1, \ldots, D.$$

(3)

When the sample in the areas of interest is of limited size, estimators such as (2) and (3) cannot be used. For example, direct estimates computed using Italian EU-SILC data have large errors at provincial level and they may not even be computable at municipality level, since many municipalities are not included in the survey sample.

In these cases small area estimation techniques are employed. The idea of small area methods is to use statistical models to link the survey variable of interest with covariate information that is also known for out of sample units. For example, to estimate the mean of the equivalised household income or some poverty indicators in the areas of interest, EU-SILC data are used to estimate statistical models while census data are used to predict the values of the target variable for the out of sample households. It follows that we can use only those variables that are common between EU-SILC and census data.

The population small area mean can be written as

$$m_d = N_d^{-1} \left(\sum_{j \in s_d} y_{jd} + \sum_{j \in r_d} y_{jd} \right), \tag{4}$$

where r_d denotes the $N_d - n_d$ non-sampled units in area d. Since the y values for the r_d non-sampled units are unknown, they need to be predicted.

Random effects models are a popular tool for small area estimation as they include random area effects to account for between area variations (Rao 2003). Referring to the decomposition (4), the Empirical Best Linear Unbiased Predictor (EBLUP) of the mean of y in small area d is:

$$\hat{m}_d^{EBLUP} = N_d^{-1} \left[\sum_{j \in s_d} y_{jd} + \sum_{j \in r_d} (\mathbf{x}_{jd}^T \hat{\beta} + \mathbf{z}_{jd}^T \hat{\gamma}_d) \right] \tag{5}$$

where $\mathbf{x}_{jd}$ is a vector of auxiliary variables known for each population unit j in small area d, $\mathbf{z}_{jd}$ is a vector of known constants, $\hat{\beta}$ and $\hat{\gamma}_d$ are Restricted Maximum Likelihood estimators of β and γ_d. See Rao (2003) for further details on the EBLUP estimator.

For the estimation of small area FGT poverty indicators, Molina and Rao (2010) have proposed a new approach. Consider the decomposition of the FGT indicators:

$$F_{\alpha d} = N_d^{-1} \left(\sum_{j \in s_d} F_{\alpha j d} + \sum_{j \in r_d} F_{\alpha j d} \right) \tag{6}$$

where $\sum_{j \in r_d} F_{\alpha j d}$ is unknown and needs to be predicted. An EBP of $F_{\alpha j d}, j \in r_d$ based on the nested error model is:

$$F_{\alpha d}^{EB} = N_d^{-1} \left(\sum_{j \in s_d} F_{\alpha j d} + \sum_{j \in r_d} \hat{F}_{\alpha j d}^{EB} \right), \tag{7}$$

where $\hat{F}_{\alpha j d}^{EB}$ is estimated using a Monte Carlo procedure. The RMSE of $F_{\alpha d}^{EB}$ can be estimated with a parametric bootstrap approach. For details see Molina and Rao (2010).

An alternative approach to small area estimation that relaxes the parametric assumptions of random effects models underlining the EBLUP and EBP approaches was proposed by Chambers and Tzavidis (2006) and Tzavidis et al. (2010). Under their setting, employing M-quantile models, the small area mean estimator is obtained using the Chambers and Dunstan (1996) distribution function estimator (CD hereafter), as shown in Tzavidis et al. (2010). The MQ/CD estimator of the small area mean, always referring to the decomposition (4), is

$$m_d^{MQ/CD} = N_j^{-1} \left\{ \sum_{j \in s_d} y_{jd} + \sum_{j \in r_d} \mathbf{x}_{jd}^T \hat{\beta}_{\psi}(\hat{\theta}_d) + \frac{N_d - n_d}{n_d} \sum_{j \in s_d} [y_{jd} - \mathbf{x}_{jd}^T \hat{\beta}_{\psi}(\hat{\theta}_d)] \right\}, \tag{8}$$

which is based on the linear M-quantile model

$$y_{jd} = \mathbf{x}_{jd}^T \hat{\beta}_\psi (q_{jd}).$$ (9)

Here ψ is the influence function associated with the qth M-quantile and the estimate $\hat{\beta}_\psi (q_{jd})$ of $\beta_\psi (q_{jd})$ is obtained, for specified q and continuous ψ, via an iterative weighted least squares algorithm. In estimator (8), $\hat{\theta}_d$ is an estimate of the average value of the M-quantile coefficients of the units in area d. See Chambers and Tzavidis (2006) and Tzavidis et al. (2010) for further details. Estimation of the MSE of estimator (8) can be achieved by using a linearization approach or a bootstrap approach as proposed by Tzavidis et al. (2010).

The M-quantile approach to small area estimation can be used also to estimate the FGT poverty indicators. Referring to the decomposition (6), the question again is how to estimate the out of sample component in that expression. This can be achieved using the same ideas described above for estimating the small area mean under the M-quantile small area model. Indeed, the estimation of poverty indicators is a special case of the quantile estimation since we are interested in estimating the number of individuals/households below a threshold. As a result, one approach to the estimation of the $F_{\alpha d}$ is the usage of a smearing-type estimator of the distribution function such as the CD estimator. In this case, an estimator $\hat{F}_{\alpha d}^{MQ}$ of $F_{\alpha d}^{MQ}$ is

$$\hat{F}_{\alpha d}^{MQ} = N_d^{-1} \left\{ \sum_{j \in s_d} I(y_{jd} \le t) + \sum_{k \in r_d} n_d^{-1} \sum_{j \in s_d} I(\hat{y}_{kd} + (y_{jd} - \hat{y}_{jd}) \le t) \right\},$$ (10)

that can be computed using a Monte Carlo procedure described in Pratesi et al. (2010), which is similar to that proposed by Molina and Rao (2010).

The M-quantile approach to poverty estimation does not require strong distributional assumptions and, because it is in some sense automatically robust to the presence of outlying observations, it can be applied directly to raw income data. On the other hand, the EBP approach attempts to minimize the effect of potential outliers in the data by modeling a transformation of the outcome variable (income or consumption). This transformation aims at satisfying the Gaussian assumptions of the random effects model employed by the EBP. However, using real data it could be difficult to find a transformation that satisfies these assumptions. Moreover, modeling a transformed variable requires a back-transformation of the small area estimates. Simple back-transformation, however, can introduce bias in the final estimates (Chambers and Dorfman 2003).

4 Estimation of Poverty Indicators at Provincial Level in Tuscany

In Italy, the EU-SILC is conducted yearly by ISTAT to produce estimates on the living conditions of the population at the national and regional (NUTS-2) levels.

Regions are planned domains for which EU-SILC estimates are published, while the provinces are unplanned domains as well as municipalities, that are partitions of the provinces. The regional samples are based on a stratified two stage sample design: in each province the municipalities are the Primary Sampling Units (PSUs), while the households are the Secondary Sampling Units (SSUs). The PSUs are divided into strata according to their dimension in terms of population size; the SSUs are selected by means of systematic sampling in each PSU. All the members of each sampled household are interviewed through an individual questionnaire, and one individual in each household (usually, the head of the household) is interviewed through a household questionnaire. It is useful to note that some provinces, generally the smaller ones, may have very few sampled municipalities; furthermore, many municipalities are not even included in the sample at all. Direct estimates may therefore have large errors at provincial level or they may not even be computable at municipality level, thereby requiring resort to small area estimation techniques.

Applying the small area methodologies presented in Sect. 3 to data from the EU-SILC 2008 survey requires covariate information that is also known for every non sampled household in the population. This information is available from the 2001 Population Census of Italy. We use these data under the hypothesis that the time lag of seven years between EU-SILC and census data does not play a determinant role on the estimates. Empirical results support this hypothesis (Pratesi et al. 2011). As an alternative, updated local administrative databases could be used. The population census of Italy has a very comprehensive questionnaire, collecting information on each household and on each individual living in the Italian territory. For the purpose of obtaining estimates on poverty and living conditions in Tuscany we selected census variables that are also available from the EU-SILC survey. These variables were included as covariates in the working small area models used for estimating the mean household income and the poverty indicators. Thus, we can say that the EU-SILC datasets, together with data coming from the Population Census of Italy, represent a complete and valuable source of information that can be used for applying advanced small area estimation techniques for producing poverty and living condition estimates in Italy.[2]

More in details, in the working small area models employed for the present application the equivalised household income is the outcome variable. To apply the EBP poverty estimators the equivalised household income values were transformed using the logarithm transformation, following Molina and Rao (2010). Covariate variables include information referring to the head of the household, namely gender, age,

---

[2] As a remark, it is important to underline that EU-SILC and census data are confidential. These data were provided by ISTAT, the Italian National Institute of Statistics, to the researchers of the SAMPLE project and were analysed for the present analysis respecting all confidentiality restrictions.

Table 1 Estimated mean of household equivalised income (Mean), Head Count Ratio (HCR), Poverty Gap (PG) and estimated Root Mean Squared Error (RMSE) for Tuscany Provinces. EBLUP and EBP estimators

Province	n	N	Mean (RMSE)	HCR % (RMSE)	PG % (RMSE)
Massa-Carrara (MS)	105	80810	16126.82(903.34)	30.1(0.8)	10.6(0.9)
Lucca (LU)	150	146117	17565.66(821.44)	24.9(1.1)	8.3(1.1)
Pistoia (PT)	136	104466	19221.09(842.15)	18.2(0.9)	5.6(1.5)
Florence (FI)	415	376255	19741.77(556.24)	18.4(1.6)	5.6(1.7)
Livorno (LI)	105	133729	17211.36(896.60)	21.9(0.4)	7.1(1.2)
Pisa (PI)	149	150259	19046.81(820.28)	18.1(1.9)	5.5(1.0)
Arezzo (AR)	143	123880	19094.15(826.36)	19.2(0.9)	5.9(0.9)
Siena (SI)	104	101399	18705.96(898.25)	18.9(1.5)	5.8(1.4)
Grosseto (GR)	65	87720	17173.97(997.23)	25.8(1.6)	8.7(1.4)
Prato (PO)	123	83617	19167.89(851.97)	16.6(1.4)	4.9(0.9)

Table 2 Estimated mean of household equivalised income (Mean), Head Count Ratio (HCR), Poverty Gap (PG) and estimated Root Mean Squared Error (RMSE) for Tuscany Provinces. M-quantile CD estimators

Province	n	N	Mean (RMSE)	HCR % (RMSE)	PG % (RMSE)
Massa-Carrara (MS)	105	80810	14964.67 (726.68)	22.1(2.7)	9.5(1.6)
Lucca (LU)	150	146117	16938.89 (816.12)	17.4(1.9)	7.0(1.0)
Pistoia (PT)	136	104466	19656.66(1050.74)	14.3(1.7)	5.4(0.9)
Florence (FI)	415	376255	20034.46 (583.18)	13.2(1.1)	5.0(0.6)
Livorno (LI)	105	133729	17117.40 (765.61)	18.5(2.1)	7.6(1.2)
Pisa (PI)	149	150259	19148.60 (842.12)	13.3(1.5)	5.0(0.8)
Arezzo (AR)	143	123880	19567.00(1066.93)	14.6(1.6)	5.6(0.9)
Siena (SI)	104	101399	19073.40(1036.51)	13.9(1.7)	5.3(0.9)
Grosseto (GR)	65	87720	17638.67(1473.16)	19.4(2.6)	8.1(1.5)
Prato (PO)	123	83617	19342.88 (855.94)	12.4(1.7)	4.5(0.9)

occupational status, civil status and years in education, and information referring to the household, that is ownership of the house, surface of the house and family size.

The results (point and MSE estimation) from the application of the EBLUP/EBP and MQ/CD estimators are presented in Tables 1 and 2. The poverty line used for the HCR and PG indicators is set to 9,300 Euros, which corresponds to 60 % of the Italian median equivalised household income, computed using EU-SILC 2008 income values referring to the whole Italian sample of households.

A first result stemming from the analysis are the higher HCR estimates obtained with the EBP estimator with respect to the MQ/CD estimator. The results referring to the mean household equivalised income and to the PG are instead more similar. Investigating the HCR estimation procedure we discovered that EBP estimates are influenced by the log-transformation: in particular, income values predicted in the log scale in the tails of the income distribution become extreme values when transformed

Table 3 Direct estimates of the mean of household equivalised income (Mean), Head Count Ratio (HCR), Poverty Gap (PG) and corresponding estimated Root Mean Squared Error (RMSE) for the Tuscany Provinces

Province	n	N	Mean (RMSE)	HCR % (RMSE)	PG % (RMSE)
Massa-Carrara (MS)	105	80810	15979.17 (721.06)	18.5(4.0)	4.3(1.3)
Lucca (LU)	150	146117	17537.98 (868.42)	17.1(3.4)	4.9(1.4)
Pistoia (PT)	136	104466	19223.72(1138.23)	14.8(3.5)	4.8(1.7)
Florence (FI)	415	376255	20395.43 (765.40)	12.4(1.9)	4.7(1.0)
Livorno (LI)	105	133729	17855.85 (884.22)	10.4(3.2)	2.6(0.9)
Pisa (PI)	149	150259	19472.92 (889.74)	11.0(2.7)	4.4(1.5)
Arezzo (AR)	143	123880	20693.88(1160.17)	8.6(2.3)	1.8(0.6)
Siena (SI)	104	101399	20975.84(1563.92)	12.2(3.7)	2.9(1.4)
Grosseto (GR)	65	87720	18595.70(1517.43)	19.1(5.2)	6.7(2.5)
Prato (PO)	123	83617	19587.26(1041.27)	7.4(3.1)	1.2(0.5)

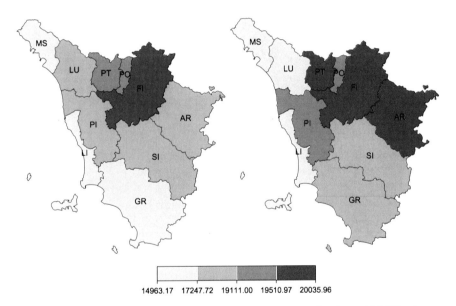

14963.17   17247.72   19111.00   19510.97   20035.96

Fig. 1 Estimated mean of household equivalised income for Tuscany Provinces. EBLUP estimator (*left*) and M-quantile CD estimator (*right*)

back using the exponential function. Where estimated income values are lower in the left tail of the income distribution, the corresponding percentages of poor households in the areas become larger. This effect of the log-transformation has instead less influence on the mean of the income distribution and on the computation of the PG. This result suggests to better investigate the effects of the log-transformation, especially in real data applications.

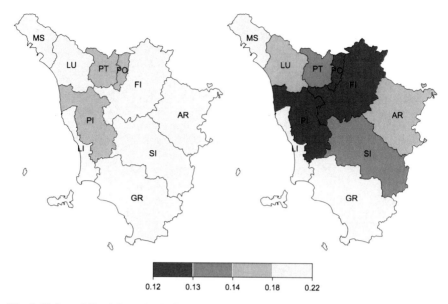

Fig. 2 Estimated Head Count Ratio for Tuscany Provinces. EBP estimator (*left*) and M-quantile CD estimator (*right*)

Given these differences, we can anyway draw some interesting conclusions on the poverty situation in Tuscany provinces. Indeed, the estimates of the mean income and of the poverty indicators in the provinces show intra-regional differences that would be lost if the scope of the analysis is limited to the regional level. In particular, we can say that the Province of Massa-Carrara has the lowest estimated mean household income, the highest percentage of poor individuals (highest HCR under both models) and the highest intensity of poverty (highest PG under both models). At the opposite the Province of Prato is characterized by the lower HCR and PG estimates. The gap between other provincial estimates is less evident, especially if the root mean square error (RMSE) estimates are considered.

We also computed the direct estimates of the mean of household equivalised income, the HCR and the PG for each province of the Tuscany Region. Results are shown in Table 3. The same estimates have also been computed for Tuscany as a whole: the direct estimate of the mean of household equivalised income is 19432.31 Euros (with RMSE equal to 353.07), the HCR is 12.7 % (with RMSE equal to 1.0) and the PG is 4.0 % (with RMSE equal to 0.4).

The direct estimates of the HCR show a high root mean squared error, while this is less evident for the mean estimates. The PG direct estimates are influenced by the HCR values, since the PG is computed selecting the households under the poverty line. Of course, conducting the analysis at a more detailed geographical level, for example using the municipalities as small areas, we would observe a higher RMSE for the direct estimates that refers to sampled municipalities. On the opposite, direct estimates referring to the Tuscany Region as a whole show acceptable RMSEs, being

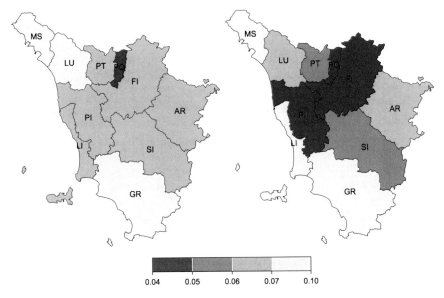

Fig. 3 Estimated Poverty Gap for Tuscany Provinces. EBP estimator (*left*) and M-quantile CD estimator (*right*)

based on a total of 1,495 sample units; indeed, regions are planned domains for the Italian EU-SILC survey.

A more effective representation of the computed poverty estimates is in Figs. 1, 2 and 3. In each figure, the map on the left was obtained with the EBLUP or EBP estimator, while that on the right refers to the corresponding MQ/CD estimator. In each map provinces are grouped in four different classes of colors, where a darker color corresponds to a better situation, namely a higher mean household income or a lower HCR and PG. To allow visual comparisons between the maps, the values chosen to define the four classes of colors for each couple of maps are the same, namely the quartiles of the corresponding MQ/CD estimates. In Figs. 2 and 3 the prevalence of lightest areas in maps showing EBP estimates is not a surprise, given the already commented HCR results.

The representation of the results by means of poverty mapping underlines the importance of computing different poverty indicators to correctly depict the living conditions in the areas of interest. In particular, it is interesting to accompany the estimation of the HCR with that of the PG. Indeed, the HCR is useful to detect the areas with higher percentages of poor households, while the PG helps to detect the areas where the intensity of poverty is lower. Thus, the PG gives an interesting indication to policy makers, since it suggests in which areas the incidence of poverty, as measured by the HCR, could be reduced more easily.

5 Conclusions

In this paper we presented several estimators to compute poverty indicators at the small area level, under the random effects models and the M-quantile approaches. The mean household equivalised income, the HCR and the PG are important estimates to study the living conditions and the poverty situation in a given area. Detailed information at local level can be used efficiently by the policy makers to develop "ad-hoc" interventions against poverty. It is important to accompany the small area estimates with a measure of their variability. For this reason, for each point estimator we also presented an estimator for the corresponding root mean squared error.

The application using EU-SILC and Census data referring to Tuscany province showed the potentialities of the EBLUP/EBP and MQ/CD estimators to obtain accurate estimates at provincial level. Future developments will focus on the estimation at a more detailed geographical level, such as the municipality level.

The MQ/CD estimators of poverty indicators presented here are in some sense automatically robust against outlier observations. However, robust EBLUP (Sinha and Rao 2009) and robust M-quantile estimators (Giusti et al. 2011) have been recently proposed to take into account the role played by outlying values. On the other hand, it would be also important to propose a robust version of the EBP poverty estimators, avoiding the need to use the log-transformation of the income values, since the back-transformation can impact the final estimates. The application of robust estimators to data coming from the EU-SILC survey could be the focus of future analysis.

Finally, further interesting developments of the present study will regard the computation at the small area level of non-monetary measures of poverty, such as fuzzy poverty indicators (Pratesi et al. 2010), to get a more complete picture of the poverty situation in the areas of interest.

Acknowledgments This work was financially supported by the European Project SAMPLE "Small Area Methods for Poverty and Living Condition Estimates", European Commission 7th FP—http://www.sample-project.eu

References

Brandolini, A., & Saraceno, C.: Introduzione. In A. Brandolini, C. Saraceno (Eds.) *Povertá e Benessere. Una Geografia delle Disuguaglianze in Italia*. Bologna: Il Mulino.

Chambers, R. L., & Dorfman, A. H. (2003). Transformed variables in survey sampling. *S3RI Methodology Working Papers* M03/21, Southampton Statistical Sciences Research Institute, University of Southampton, UK.

Chambers, R. L., & Dunstan, R. (1996). Estimating distribution functions from survey data. *Biometrika, 73*, 597–604.

Chambers, R. L., & Tzavidis, N. (2006). M-quantile models for small area estimation. *Biometrika, 93*, 255–268.

Cheli, B., & Lemmi, A. (1995). A totally fuzzy and relative approach to the multidimensional analysis of poverty. *Economic Notes, 24*, 115–134.

Elbers, C., Lanjouw, J. O., & Lanjouw, P. (2003). Micro-level estimation of poverty and inequality. *Econometrica, 71*, 355–364.

Eurostat. (2007). *Description of SILC user database variables.* Version 2007.1 from 01–03-2009. Eurostat.

Foster, J., Greer, J., & Thorbecke, E. (1984). A class of decomposable poverty measures. *Econometrica, 52*, 761–766.

Giusti, C., Tzavidis, N., Pratesi, M., & Salvati, N.: Resistance to outliers of M-quantile and robust random effects small area models. *S3RI Methodology Working Papers* M11/04, Southampton Statistical Sciences Research Institute, University of Southampton, UK.

ISTAT. (2008). L'indagine europea sui redditi e le condizioni di vita delle famiglie (Eu-Silc). *Metodi e Norme, 37.*

ISTAT. (2010). *noi Italia. 100 statistiche per capire il Paese in cui viviamo.* ISTAT.

Molina, I., & Rao, J. N. K. (2010). Small area estimation of poverty indicators. *Canadian Journal of Statistics, 38*, 369–385.

Pratesi, M., Giusti, C., Marchetti, S., & Salvati, N. (2011). Robust small area estimation of poverty indicators. In *Survey research methods and applications*, pp. 17–20. Pisa: Edizioni Plus.

Pratesi, M., Giusti, C., Marchetti, S., Salvati, N., Tzavidis, N., Molina, I., Durbán, M., Grané, A., Marín, J. M., Veiga, M. H., Morales, D., Esteban, M. D., Sánchez, A., Santamaría, L., Marhuenda, Y., Pérez, A., Pagliarella, M. C., Rao, J. N. K., & Ferretti, C. (2010). *Sample Deliverables 12 and 16. Final small area estimation developments and simulations results.* http://www.sample-project.eu/it/the-project/deliverables-docs.html

Rao, J. N. K. (2003). *Small area estimation.* New York: Wiley.

Sinha, S. K., & Rao, J. N. K. (2009). Robust small area estimation. *Canadian Journal of Statistics, 37*, 381–399.

Tzavidis, N., Marchetti, S., & Chambers, R. (2010). Robust prediction of small area means and distributions. *Australian and New Zealand Journal of Statistics, 52*, 167–186.

Non-Sampling Errors in Household Surveys: The Bank of Italy's Experience

Giovanni D'Alessio and Giuseppe Ilardi

Abstract Non-sampling errors are a serious problem in household surveys. This paper exploits the Bank of Italy's Survey on Household Income and Wealth to show how these issues can be studied and how the main effects on estimates can be accounted for. The topics examined are unit non-response, uncorrelated measurement errors and some specific cases of underreporting. The unit non-response can be overcome by weighting valid cases using external (typically demographic and geographical) information or by modelling the respondents' propensities to participate in the survey. The effect of the uncorrelated measurement errors can be evaluated using specific reliability indices constructed with the information collected over the panel component. The underreporting bias of income and wealth is estimated by combining statistical matching techniques with auxiliary information and by exploiting different response behaviours across different groups.

1 Introduction

Errors in survey data can be divided depending on the source into two broad categories: sampling and non-sampling errors. The former includes errors in estimating the relevant population parameters derived from the inferential process: these tend to vanish as the sample size increases. Non-sampling errors mainly relate to measurement design, data collection and processing.

Non-sampling errors comprise quite diverse specific types of error that are usually harder to control than sampling ones. Following Biemer and Lyberg (2003), we can classify the non-sampling errors as: specification error; coverage or frame error;

G. D'Alessio (✉) and G. Ilardi
Bank of Italy, Economic and Financial Statistics Department, Rome, Italy
e-mail: giovanni.dalessio@bancaditalia.it

G. Ilardi
e-mail: giuseppe.ilardi@bancaditalia.it

C. Davino and L. Fabbris (eds.), *Survey Data Collection and Integration*,
DOI: 10.1007/978-3-642-21308-3_7, © Springer-Verlag Berlin Heidelberg 2013

processing error; unit non-response; and measurement errors.[1] Usually non-sampling errors affect both bias and the variance of estimators; and their effects do not necessarily diminish as sample size increases. In many economic applications, the non-sampling component of total error outweighs the sampling one.[2] This is the case in many of the variables collected in the Bank of Italy's Survey of Household Income and Wealth (SHIW). The survey estimate of total household net wealth is approximately half the corresponding value deriving from the financial accounts (FA). True, the FA data rely on many measurement hypotheses and are subject to errors; nevertheless this discrepancy cannot be attributed to sample variability and is likely to depend on non-sampling errors—presumably because of a lower propensity of wealthier households to participate in the survey and/or widespread underreporting by respondents of their assets. This evidence is the Bank of Italy's strongest motivation for its efforts to analyse non-sampling errors for the household budget survey. In the next sections we evaluate non-sampling errors that typically occur in the SHIW. This informal approach allows the discussion of some of the typical problems associated with using household data.[3]

After a brief description of the SHIW (Sect. 2), we describe the survey experiences with non-response (Sect. 3.1), measurement errors (Sect. 3.2) and underreporting (Sect. 3.3). Section 4 concludes.

2 The Survey on Household Income and Wealth

Since 1965, the SHIW gathers data on Italian households' income, wealth, consumption and use of payment instruments. It was conducted annually until 1984 and biannually since (with the exception of 1998). The sample consists of about 8,000 households (secondary units) in 350 municipalities (primary units), drawn from a population of approximately 24 million households. The primary units are stratified by region and municipality size. Within each stratum, the selected municipalities include all those with a population of more than 40,000 units (self-representing municipalities), while the smaller towns are selected with probability proportional

---

[1] A specification error occurs when the collected data do not include relevant economic variables for the survey objectives. A coverage error exists when some statistical units belonging to the reference population are not included in the sampling frame. Non-response errors occur because some households do not participate in the survey. Measurement errors arise during the data collection process; errors made by the interviewer or by the respondent, and the mode of data collection contribute to measurement error. Processing errors include errors emerging from data entry, computer programs (i.e. miscalculation of the weights) or incomplete instructions. An alternative classification distinguishes non-sampling errors on the base of the source of such errors; for instance, the interviewer may affect both unit non-response, item non-response and measurement errors (Blom 2011).

[2] In budgeting a survey there is a clear trade-off between the two types of error. Resources can be devoted to procuring a large sample and thus minimizing random sampling errors or else concentrated on a smaller sample but with better interviewer controls, a higher response rate and more accurate data collection procedures.

[3] See Lessler and Kalsbeek (1992) for a general exposition on non-sampling errors.

to size. At the second stage, the individual households are selected randomly from the population register.[4,5] Through 1987 the survey used time-independent samples (cross sections) of households. In order to facilitate the analysis of changes, the 1989 survey introduced a panel component, and almost half of the sample now consists of households interviewed in one or more previous waves. Data are collected by a market research institute through computer-assisted personal interviews. Households answer an electronic questionnaire—that not only stores data but also performs a number of checks so that data inconsistencies can be remedied directly in the presence of the respondent. The Bank of Italy publishes a regular report with the main results, the text of the questionnaire and the main methodological choices. Anonymized microdata and full documentation can be accessed online for research purposes only (microdata are available from 1977 onwards). Recent economic studies based on this survey have covered such topics as households' real and financial assets over time; risk aversion, wealth and financial market imperfections; dynamics of wealth accumulation; payment instruments used; and tax evasion. The financial section has been extensively exploited for studies on the financial structure of the Italian economy. The SHIW is also part of the European household survey promoted by the euro-area national central banks in order to gather harmonized data on income and wealth.

3 Unit Non-Response and Measurement Errors in the SHIW: Some Empirical Studies

3.1 The Analysis of Unit Non-Response

In most household surveys not all the units selected will participate. The difference between the intended and the actual sample reflects both unwillingness to participate (refusals) and other reasons (most commonly, "not at home"). This may have serious consequences for survey statistics, which need to be properly addressed. Let us consider the case of units that are selected to be surveyed but do not participate. Denoting by y_r the values of variable y for the group of n_r respondents and by y_{nr} the values for the unobserved group of $n - n_r$ non-respondents, the estimator of the mean can be decomposed into two parts

$$\bar{y} = \frac{n_r}{n} \bar{y}_r + \frac{n - n_r}{n} \bar{y}_{nr}. \tag{1}$$

---

[4] Since households are extracted from the registry lists, the reference population does not include Italian citizens living in institutions (prisons, barracks, nursing homes or convents).

[5] Respondents receive a participation letter explaining the purpose of the survey, a booklet describing the main uses of the information and a small gift; a toll-free telephone number is available to supply any information about the survey.

The expected value of $\bar{y}$ is given by $\mu = f\mu_r + (1 - f)\mu_{nr}$, where f is the response rate, i.e. the share of responding units in the population, and μ_r and μ_{nr} are the population means of the responding and non-responding units respectively.

The estimator computed on respondents only, $\bar{y}_r$, is a biased estimator of μ, with a bias given by

$$E(\bar{y}_r) - \mu = (1 - f)(\mu_r - \mu_{nr}). \tag{2}$$

The magnitude of non-response bias depends both on the non-response rate $1 - f$ and on the difference between μ_r and μ_{nr}. When non-response occurs, the estimator $\bar{y}_r$ will be biased unless the pattern of non-response is random, that is the assumption $\mu_r = \mu_{nr}$ holds.

In household surveys, however, we cannot assume that non-responses are totally random; both the sample units that refuse to participate and those that are not at home tend to belong to specific population groups; so we need a procedure to correct for the bias.[6]

If we knew the participation probability p_i of household i, an unbiased estimator of the population mean could be obtained by extending the Horvitz–Thompson estimator (Little and Rubin 1987)

$$\bar{y} = \frac{\sum_{i=1}^{n} w_i y_i}{\sum_{i=1}^{n} w_i}, \tag{3}$$

where $w_i = 1/(\pi_i p_i)$, to include both the probability of being included in the sample π_i and the probability of actually participating p_i.[7] We assume that these two sets of weighting coefficients are independent of each other. In order to correct for non-response, we need information on the selection process governing the response behaviour. But how can we obtain information on this process, given that non-respondents—by definition—are not reached by interviewers or deliberately avoid participation?

Several statistical techniques, based on various assumptions, can be employed. Knowledge of the distribution of some relevant characteristics for the entire population allows us to compare the sample with the corresponding census data. A significant deviation of the sample distribution from that of the population gives us indirect information on the selection process. The sample composition can thus be aligned with the population distributions by means of post-stratification techniques.[8]

---

[6] See Särndal and Lundström (2005) for a recent review of estimation methods to account for non-response.

[7] Many practitioners believe that the purpose of weighting is to reduce non-response bias, at the cost of increasing the variance of the estimates and transforming the efficacy of weighting adjustments into a bias-variance trade-off. However, Little and Vartivarian (2005) point out that if the weighting adjustments are positively correlated with the survey outcome, then the weighting system can also reduce sampling variance of the estimates.

[8] When only marginals are known, the technique employed is called as Iterative Proportional Fitting or Raking (Kalton and Flores Cervantes 2003). More in general, the calibration techniques, based on the linear regression model, offer a wide variety of solutions in adjusting the sample weights so

The SHIW data show a higher frequency of elderly persons than the census of the population, while younger persons are underrepresented. Post-stratification is a common practice of embedding into estimators information about population structure; the procedure can also reduce the variability of the estimates. Unfortunately, the information available for post-stratification is often limited (sex, age, education, region, town size) and as such is insufficient for a complete detection of non-response behaviour.

As a part of the SHIW sample consists of households already interviewed in past waves (the panel component), information on the propensity to participate can be obtained by an analysis of attrition, i.e. non-participation of a panel household in a subsequent wave of the survey. Following this approach, Cannari and D'Alessio (1993) found that non-response characterizes households in urban areas and in the northern Italy; and that participation rates decline as income rises and household size decreases. The relationship with the age of the head of household is more ambiguous: not-at-homes decline sharply with age but refusals and other forms of non-participation increase. On the basis of these findings, Cannari and D'Alessio estimated that non-participation caused a 5.4 % underestimate of household income in 1989.

This approach cannot be considered fully satisfactory; in fact, its validity depends on the assumption that the pattern of attrition within the panel component can be assimilated to non-participation of households contacted for the first time. Actually, a household's decision to participate in the survey may have been influenced by a previous interview and the estimation of the attrition pattern can shed light only on some aspects of non-response.

In many cases, some characteristics of non-respondents can be detected. In conducting personal interviews, for example, the characteristics of the neighbourhood and of the building are observable. In the most recent SHIW waves, several sorts of information on non-respondents have been gathered. Comparing respondents and non-respondents as regards these characteristics can help us understand the possible bias arising from non-response.

Information on the characteristics of non-respondents can also be inferred by analyzing the effort required to get the interview from responding households. The survey report usually includes a table with the number of contacts needed to obtain an interview, according to the characteristics of the households. In 2008, in order to get 7,977 interviews a total of 14,839 contacts was attempted (Banca d'Italia 2010b).[9] The difficulty of obtaining an interview increased with income, wealth and the educational attainment of the household head. It was easier to get interviews

---

(Footnote 8 continued)

as to reproduce ancillary external known information. Singh and Mohl (1996) provide a detailed description of many of these methods.

[9] The households that could not be interviewed were replaced by others selected randomly in the same municipality.

in smaller municipalities, with smaller households and with households headed by retired persons or women.[10]

We can compare the households interviewed at first visit with those that have been interviewed after both an initial refusal or a failure in the contact (not at home). These two groups offer valuable information on non-response. The households successfully interviewed after first being found not-at-home and that who initially refused to participate appear to have a higher income and wealth than the average sample (for the two groups, by 5.0 and 21.6% for income and by 5.5 and 27.1% for wealth respectively).

Assuming that the households interviewed after an initial not-at-home or after a refusal can provide useful information on non-responding units, we can estimate the bias due to non-response. An adjusted estimate can be obtained by re-weighting the interviewed households by the inverse of their propensity to participate. The results for the 1998 survey (D'Alessio and Faiella 2002) showed that wealthier households had a lower propensity to participate in the SHIW. Thus the adjusted estimates of income and wealth are higher than the unadjusted estimates. The correction is smaller for income and for real wealth, more significant for financial assets (ranging respectively from 7 to 14%, 8 to 21% and 15 to 31 %, depending on the model adopted).[11]

Different estimates of the effects of unit non-response on sample estimates were obtained by a specific experiment carried out in the 1998 survey. A supplementary sample of about 2,000 households, customers of a leading commercial bank, was contacted, 513 of which were actually interviewed.[12] For these out-of-sample households, the SHIW gathered data on actual financial assets held, the results of the current and supplementary samples were similar.[13]

3.2 Measurement Errors: Uncorrelated Errors

One of the most important sources of error in sample surveys is the discrepancy between the recorded and the "true" micro-data. These inconsistencies may be due to response errors or to oversights in the processing phase prior to estimation.

[10] In the most recent wave, the Bank of Italy conducted an experiment aiming to evaluate the effect of the gift on the participation.

[11] D'Alessio and Faiella's method belongs to the class of sequential weight adjustment (Groves and Couper 1998; Iannacchione 2003) which constructs the non-response adjustment weights by modelling the information on the two-stage response process, contact and participation. A different class of non-response adjustment that can be used in a regression analysis is the sample selection models (Heckman 1979). In this framework, the economic relation of interest is modelled with an additional regression equation that account for the censoring of non-participating households. In this strand of literature, a recent work by De Luca and Peracchi (2011) proposes an adjustment procedure both for the item and the unit non-response using semiparametric inference.

[12] The supplementary sample was drawn from a list of clients following a stratified random sample method, with a higher sampling rate for wealthier households.

[13] A strict protocol was devised to guarantee full protection of the respondents' confidentiality.

Irrespective of the reasons, the effects of errors on estimates are seldom negligible, so we need to evaluate their size and causes.

Involuntary errors in reporting values of some phenomena (e.g. the size of one's dwellings), due to rounding or to lack of precise knowledge, may still cause serious problems for estimators.

Consider a continuous variable X measured with an additive error: $Y = X + \varepsilon$. The measure Y differs from the true value X by a random component with the following properties: $E(\varepsilon) = 0$; $E(X, \varepsilon) = \sigma_{X,\varepsilon} = 0$; $E(\varepsilon^2) = \sigma_\varepsilon^2$. This type of disturbance is called homoscedastic and with uncorrelated measurement error. Under these assumptions, the average of Y is an unbiased estimator of the unobservable variable X–as $E(Y) = E(X)$–while the variance of Y is a biased estimator of the variance of X. In fact

$$\sigma_Y^2 = \sigma_X^2 + \sigma_\varepsilon^2 = \frac{\sigma_X^2}{\lambda^2}, \tag{4}$$

where $\lambda^2 = \sigma_X^2/\sigma_Y^2$ is the reliability coefficient. Therefore, the index λ is the ratio of the X and Y variances (Lord and Novick 1968).[14]

Under these assumptions, we can determine the equivalent size of a sample, i.e. the size that would yield the same variance of the sample mean if there were no measurement error: $n^* = \lambda^2 \cdot n$. If there were no error, equally precise estimates could be obtained with smaller samples (for instance, by 36%, $(1 - \lambda^2)$, with a reliability index $\lambda = 0.8$).

In correlation analysis, if measurement error on X is assumed to be uncorrelated with X and with another variable Z, measured free of error, then the correlation coefficient between X and Z is attenuated with intensity proportional to the reliability index of Y: $\rho_{Y,Z} = \lambda_Y \rho_{X,Z}$. If Z is also measured with error, $W = Z + \eta$, with the η error of the same type as above and uncorrelated with ε, the correlation coefficient is attenuated even more: $\rho_{Y,W} = \lambda_Y \lambda_W \rho_{X,Z}$. In simple regression analysis too, measurement errors in independent variables lead to a downward bias in the parameter estimates (attenuation). In a multiple-regression context, measurement errors in independent variables still produce bias, but its direction can be either upward or downward. Random measurement error in the dependent variable does not bias the slope coefficients but does lead to larger standard errors.

The foregoing makes it clear that even unbiased and uncorrelated measurement errors may produce serious estimation problems.

How can we get a measure of the reliability of survey variables? A first possibility for time-invariant variables is the use of information collected over time on the same units (panel). In our survey half the sample is composed of panel households. If we assume that the measures of time invariant variables are independent (a plausible assumption for a survey conducted at two-year intervals), a comparison over time gives an indication of reliability.

---

[14] A reliability index evaluates the degree to which an instrument gives consistent results; "reliability" does not imply the accuracy of the measurement, i.e. its truthfulness. A reliable measurement device is not necessarily accurate, as for instance in case of correct and consistent recording of false information (Hand et al. 2001).

Let Y_s and Y_t be the values observed in two subsequent waves, with additive errors: $Y_s = X + \varepsilon_s$ and $Y_t = X + \varepsilon_t$. Under the assumptions that

$$E(\varepsilon_s, \varepsilon_t) = 0 \text{ and } E(X, \varepsilon_s) = E(X, \varepsilon_t) = 0, \quad \forall s, t = 1, \dots, T, \quad s \neq t, \quad (5)$$

the correlation coefficient between the two measurements Y_s and Y_t equals the square of the reliability index: $\rho_{Y_s, Y_t} = \lambda^2$. If there is no measurement error, the coefficient equals 1. Hence, a reduction in the precision of the data collection process or in the reliability of the respondents' answers lowers the correlation coefficient.

If we consider the surface area of the primary dwelling (computed only for households who did not move and did not incur extraordinary renovation expenses between the two survey waves), the correlation coefficient is 0.65 (and the reliability index $\lambda = 0.80$). For the year of house construction, the correlation coefficient is still lower ($\rho = 0.55$); in 73 % of the cases, the spread is less than five years, but sometimes it is much greater, probably reflecting response difficulties for houses that have been heavily renovated.

Another variable that is subject to inconsistency is the year when the respondents started working. The usual problems of recall are presumably aggravated in this instance by a certain degree of ambiguity in the question: it is not clear whether occasional jobs or training periods should be included or not. Out of 6,708 individuals who answered the question both in 2006 and 2008, 40.6 % gave answers that do not match; linear correlation was only 0.71.

All these examples underscore the great importance and the difficulty, in surveys, of framing questions to which respondents can provide reliable answers. It is not only a problem of knowledge and memory. There may also be a more general ambiguity in definitions (how to count a garden or terrace in the surface area of a house? Should the walls be included?), which can be limited (say, by instructing both interviewers and respondents) but cannot be eliminated.

Dealing with categorical variables complicates the study; in fact the models presented above are no longer adequate. An index of reliability for categorical variables can be constructed using two measures (Y_1 and Y_2) on the same set of n units. The fraction of units λ^* classified consistently is a reliability index (Biemer and Trewin 1997). Analytically, λ^* is given by

$$\lambda^* = \frac{tr(F)}{n} = \frac{\sum_{i=1}^{n} f_{ii}}{n}, \quad (6)$$

where F is the cross-tabulation of Y_1 and Y_2 whose generic element is f_{ij} and $tr(.)$ is the trace operator, i.e. the sum of the diagonal elements.

However, the index λ^* does not take account of the fact that consistent answers could be partly random: if the two measures Y_1 and Y_2 are independent random variables, the expected share of consistent units is $\sum_{i=1}^{n} f_{i.} f_{.i} / n$. A reliability index that controls for this effect is Cohen's κ (Cohen 1960) that can be obtained by normalizing the share of observed matching cases with respect to the expected share, on the assumption that the two measurements of Y_1 and Y_2 were independent

Table 1 Reliability of type of high school degree, 2006–2008. Percentages

	2008 A	B	C	D	E	F	Total
2006							
A. Vocational school	4.9	4.2	0.5	0.1	0.4	0.4	10.5
B. Technical school	4.1	44.1	2.4	0.3	0.6	1.1	52.7
C. Specialized high schools (*Licei*)	0.7	1.8	15.6	0.3	0.4	0.1	19.0
D. Art schools and institutes	0.1	0.1	0.2	2.0	0.2	0.0	2.6
E. Teacher training school	0.5	0.5	0.4	0.0	11.8	0.1	13.3
F. Other	0.3	0.5	0.4	0.0	0.2	0.4	1.9
Total	10.6	51.3	19.5	2.7	13.7	2.2	100.0
Reliability index λ^* (consistent answers)	88.7	84.2	92.7	98.7	96.6	96.7	78.8
Cohen's κ	40.1	68.4	76.5	74.8	85.4	17.8	68.0

$$\kappa = \frac{\lambda^* - \sum_{i=1}^{n} f_{i.} f_{.i}/n}{1 - \sum_{i=1}^{n} f_{i.} f_{.i}/n}. \tag{7}$$

Both λ^* and κ can also be applied to assess the reliability of all the categories of the qualitative variables, enabling us to pinpoint the main classification problems.[15]

If we compare the information on the type of high school diploma reported in the 2006 and 2008 waves, we find that about 20% of the responses differ ($\lambda^* = 78.8$, Table 1). The transition matrix shows that a large part of the inconsistencies are between vocational and technical schools (4.1 and 4.2%). In fact, the *Technical school* category reveals the lowest, but still high, reliability index $\lambda_B^* = 84.2$. However, once the correction for random consistent answers is considered the Cohen's measure of reliability turns out to be $\kappa = 68.0$. Moreover, the residual *Other* and *Vocational school* categories appear to be quite unreliable ($\kappa_F = 17.8$ and $\kappa_A = 40.1$).

Unfortunately, most of the SHIW variables vary over time, so their reliability cannot be measured by these techniques. More sophisticated instruments are required to distinguish actual changes from those induced by wrong measurements. A simple model allowing the estimation of the reliability index on time-varying quantities has been proposed by Heise (1969). The Author showed that, under mild conditions, real dynamics can be disentangled from measurement errors by taking three separate measurements of the economic variable on the same panel units.

Let X_1, X_2 and X_3 be the true unobservable values of the variable X during periods 1, 2, and 3, and Y_1, Y_2 and Y_3 be the corresponding observed measures. In order to apply the Heise method we assume that

$$Y_t = X_t + \varepsilon_t \quad \forall t = 1, 2, 3 \tag{8}$$

---

[15] Several indexes have been proposed for assessing the reliability of two or more measures (Krippendorff 2004). The so-called "weighted κ" has been proposed when the researcher may consider some disagreements less important than others (i.e. in the case of ordinal data). The Krippendorff's α is a more general index that can be applied on two or more repeated observations, on any metric (nominal, ordinal, interval, ratio), and on data with missing values (Krippendorff 2007).

and the dependency structure between X_1, X_2 and X_3 follows a first-order autoregressive model (not necessarily stationary) as

$$X_1 = \delta_1, \ X_2 = \beta_{2,1}X_1 + \delta_2, \dots, X_3 = \beta_{3,2}X_2 + \delta_3 \qquad (9)$$

where $\beta_{t,t-1}$ is the autoregressive coefficient and δ_t is a classical idiosyncratic error. We further impose that the innovation ε_t follows a white noise process and that the level of reliability of a given variable does not vary over time. On these assumptions the estimate of reliability can be derived from the following simple relation

$$\lambda^2 = \frac{\rho_{Y_1 Y_2} \rho_{Y_2 Y_3}}{\rho_{Y_1 Y_3}}. \qquad (10)$$

The intuition is that if measurement errors are independent over time and are not correlated with the underlying variable, then the absolute value of the estimated autocorrelation coefficients is lower than it would be if the observed value does not include measurement error. In fact, the method proposes an estimate of measurement reliability by comparing the product of one-step correlations $\rho_{Y_1 Y_2}$ and $\rho_{Y_2 Y_3}$ with the two-step correlation $\rho_{Y_1 Y_3}$. Without measurement error, the product $\rho_{Y_1 Y_2} \cdot \rho_{Y_2 Y_3}$ would be equal to $\rho_{Y_1 Y_3}$. As the intensity of measurement error is actually proportional to the square of $\rho_{Y_1 Y_3}$, we can derive an indicator of measurement reliability by separating out the part that the model attributes to the actual variation of the underlying quantity.

In line with Biancotti et al. (2008), Table 2 reports the reliability indexes computed on three consecutive survey waves for the main variables, starting with 1989–1991–1993 and ending with 2004–2006–2008. The reliability estimate for income (on average 0.87) is higher than for net wealth and consumption (both averaging about 0.80).[16] Among the income components, higher index numbers are found for pension and transfer and for wage and salary (both around 0.95); incomes from self-employment or capital show lower values (around 0.80). As to the wealth components, greater reliability is found for real assets (on average 0.82), and in particular for primary residences (0.90), and lesser for financial assets (0.65).

These results are useful from three different perspectives. First, they allow the many researchers who use the survey to take this aspect properly into account, i.e. by selecting, among similar economic indicators, the most reliable. This benefit may also extend to other, similar surveys, which are likely to be affected by the same issues. Second, our results can help data producers for this kind of survey to find ways of reducing this kind of error; in fact, the difficulties discussed here are not specific to the SHIW data acquisition procedures. Quantifying their impact and determining their causes are essential preliminaries to improving survey procedures. Third, our conclusions can hopefully serve as standard practice for data producers and a blueprint for quality reporting.

---

[16] As noted, a reliability index does not measure the "closeness" of the reported to the true value, but only the variability of the measure. This implies that a systematic bias (for example due to consistent underreporting) will not be reflected in the Heise index.

Table 2 Heise reliability indexes of the main variables in the SHIW, 1989–2008

	1989 1991 1993	1991 1993 1995	1993 1995 1998	1995 1998 2000	1998 2000 2002	2000 2002 2004	2002 2004 2006	2004 2006 2008	Average
Net income	**0.89**	**0.94**	**0.89**	**0.84**	**0.89**	**0.85**	**0.80**	**0.82**	**0.87**
Wages and salaries	0.97	0.98	0.96	0.94	0.94	0.94	0.91	0.95	0.95
Pensions and transfers	0.97	0.99	0.96	0.93	0.93	0.94	0.97	0.90	0.95
Income from self-employment	0.89	0.97	0.84	0.71	0.75	0.81	0.73	0.82	0.82
Income from capital	0.82	0.79	0.81	0.77	0.79	0.78	0.74	0.81	0.79
Net wealth	**0.80**	**0.74**	**0.76**	**0.87**	**0.86**	**0.82**	**0.86**	**0.85**	**0.82**
Real assets	0.80	0.72	0.73	0.88	0.89	0.82	0.89	0.85	0.82
Financial assets	0.66	0.81	0.93	0.68	0.46	0.62	0.46	0.61	0.65
Financial liabilities	0.67	0.84	0.88	0.67	0.73	0.81	0.79	0.77	0.77
Consumption	**0.85**	**0.81**	**0.79**	**0.74**	**0.82**	**0.77**	**0.76**	**0.86**	**0.80**

3.3 Measurement Errors: Underreporting

In household surveys on income and wealth, the most significant type of measurement error is the voluntary underreporting of income and wealth. This type of error can produce severe bias in estimates, and special techniques are required to overcome this effect.

To evaluate the underreporting problem, a useful approach is to compare the survey estimates with other sources of data such as the National Accounts, administrative registers, fiscal data, and other surveys. For example, the number of dwellings declared in the survey differs significantly from the number owned by households according to the census.[17] On the basis of this evidence, underreporting by households could amount to as much as 20 or 25 % of all dwellings.

Further, underreporting is not constant by type of dwelling. While owner-occupied dwellings (principal residences) appear to be always declared, underreporting of other real estate owned proves to be very substantial. The SHIW itself allows a comparison between the estimate of the total number of houses owned by households and rented to others and the corresponding estimate drawn from the number of households living in rented dwellings.[18] In practice, the underestimation here appears to be very severe, as much as 60 or 70 %.

The estimates of real and financial wealth also appear to be underestimated by comparison with the aggregate accounts (Banca d'Italia 2010a). The bias is greater for financial assets, and underreporting is larger for less commonly held assets (equity and investment fund units). This suggests that unadjusted sample estimates are biased and that this distortion is not uniform across segments of the population.

---

[17] The number of dwellings owned by individuals is taken from the most recent census and updated using data from CRESME (CRESME 2010) on new buildings (owned by natural persons).

[18] Note that owing to sampling variance, even without underreporting the two estimates, though close, should not be exactly the same (Cannari and D'Alessio 1990).

How can we learn more about this, and how can we adjust the estimates accordingly? One way of assessing the credibility of the survey responses is to ask for the interviewers' own impression. That is, in the course of the interviews they are requested to look out for additional information, making a practical comparison between the household's answers and the objective evidence they can see for themselves: type of neighbourhood and dwelling, the standard of living implied by the quality of furnishings, and so on.

In the 2008 survey, credibility is satisfactory overall (an average score of 7.6 out of 10) but not completely uniform. The highest scores are for the better educated and for payroll employees (7.9 and 7.8, respectively), the lowest for the elderly and the self-employed (7.4 and 7.3, respectively).

The correlation coefficient between the credibility score and the declared values of income, financial assets and financial liabilities is positive and significant, but small. The use of this type of information is of little help for the adjustment of the estimates. For example, considering only the sub-sample of households with credibility better than 5 (around 90% of the sample), average household income rises by just 1.1%. The adjustment is a bit larger (2.8%) considering only the households that score 7 or more. In these two cases, the wealth adjustments are respectively 0.8 and 3.2%; the adjustment for financial assets is greater (between 4 and 11%).

Taking a completely different approach, underreporting can be analysed by statistical matching procedures. Cannari et al. (1990) performed statistical matching between the SHIW answers and the data acquired by means of a specific survey conducted by a commercial bank on its customers. Under the hypothesis that the bank clients report the full amount of financial assets held, as customers are likely to trust their bank, the Authors estimated the amount of financial assets held by the households in the SHIW database.[19] The study concluded that the survey respondents tend to underreport their assets quite significantly. The underreporting involved several different components. Some households, in fact, do not declare any bank or postal accounts, and hence the ownership of financial assets is underestimated. This behaviour was determined to result in an underestimation of about 5%; it was more frequent among the poorer and less educated respondents. Underestimation due to non-reporting of single assets, i.e. the omission of assets actually held, involved a further 10% of assets. But the bulk of the underreporting concerned the amounts of the assets declared. The study found that for a declared value of 100, households actually held assets worth 170.

Applying this correction, the total amount of financial assets owned by households doubled. The discrepancy with respect to the financial accounts was sharply reduced, but a significant gap remained, presumably deriving from definitional differences and the very substantial asset holdings of the tiny group of very wealthy

---

[19] On the assumption that the probability of declaring an asset not actually held is zero, the conditional probability of not declaring an asset held is simply obtained by using marginal probability: $p_{h/nd} = 1 - (1 - p_h)/(1 - p_d)$. The marginal probabilities can be estimated on the two samples separately.

households, which are not properly represented in sample surveys. The adjustment ratio for financial assets, finally, was higher among the elderly and the self-employed.

Another matching experiment, based on the same data but with different methods (Cannari and D'Alessio 1993), confirmed the foregoing results. The experiment also showed that the Gini concentration index of household wealth was not seriously affected by the adjustment procedures (from 0.644 to 0.635 for 1991).

In a recent paper on this topic, D'Aurizio et al. (2006) use an alternative method and data drawn from a different commercial bank. On average, the adjusted estimates are more than twice the unadjusted data and equal to 85 % of the financial accounts figures. The adjustments are greatest for the households whose head is less educated or retired.

Neri and Zizza (2010) propose different approaches to correct for underreporting of household income. To adjust the estimates for self-employed households, the procedure uses the ratio of the value of the primary residence to labour income; this approach is a variant of the one proposed by Pissarides and Weber (1989), based on the ratio of food expenditure to income. The ratio of the value of homes to labour income is estimated first for public employees, whose answers are presumed not to be underreported. The estimated parameters are then applied to the self-employed (the value of houses is assumed to be reported correctly by both types of respondent). On this basis the estimated average income from self-employment is 36 % greater than the unadjusted figure. To adjust income from financial assets, the authors used the (D'Aurizio et al. 2006) methodology for the correction of financial stocks, simply applying a return rate to the adjusted capital stock. It was found that on average this adjustment tripled the reported income. The increase in liabilities was modest (just 9 %). As to the income from real estate, they used the procedure developed by Cannari and D'Alessio (1990), which adjusts the number of declared second homes to the Census. The income from actual and imputed rents increased on average by 23 %. Income sources from other labour activities was adjusted on the basis of the Italian part of the European Union Statistics on Income and Living Conditions (EU-SILC), which includes information from administrative and fiscal sources. With this adjustment, additional payroll and self-employment income increased by 3 and 4 % points respectively. Overall, the adjustment procedures produce an estimate of total family income about 12 % greater than the declared value (between 2 and 4 times the corresponding sampling errors). In summary, analysis of the discrepancy between the survey figures and the financial accounts shows the simultaneous presence of non-response, non-reporting and underreporting. The underestimation of financial assets and liabilities due to non-participation in the survey appears to be less substantial than that caused by non-reporting and underreporting.

In the 2010 survey, the SHIW tried the *unmatched count technique* (Raghavarao and Federer 1979) for eliciting honest answers on usury, a serious problem mainly for small businesses and poor households but a phenomenon on which no reliable information is available. The technique uses anonymity to get a larger number of true answers to sensitive or embarrassing questions. In this case, the respondents are randomly split into two groups, A and B. The control group B is asked to answer a set of k harmless binary questions $X_1, \ldots, X_k$, while the treatment group A has one additional question Y (the sensitive one). The respondents in both groups are to reveal only the number of applicable activities or behaviors, not to respond specifically to each item. Hence, the answers have the forms of $S_B = X_1 + X_2 + \cdots + X_k$ and $S_A = S_B + Y$ for respondents belonging to A and B group respectively. With the unmatched count, the number of people who answered "yes" to the sensitive question is estimated by comparing the two mean values: $\overline{Y} = \overline{S}_A - \overline{S}_B$. Under certain conditions, researchers can also perform regressions on this type of data.[20]

4 Concluding Remarks

This work has described the research done at the Bank of Italy on non-sampling errors in the SHIW to bring out the most common problems in household surveys. These errors are frequent and constitute the largest part of the total error. We gauge the impact of non-participation in the survey, classic measurement error and under-reporting, and describe some practical procedures for correcting these error sources. We show that the correction procedures often depend on the specific assumptions. For this reason the techniques are more in the nature of tools that a researcher can legitimately use than of standard practices for the production of descriptive statistics, such as those reported in the official Bank of Italy reports.

As survey designers, we have shown that it is simply essential to collect additional information, beyond that strictly related to the content of the survey. In the SHIW, we acquire information on: the households not interviewed; the effort needed to acquire the interviews; the time spent on the interviews; the credibility of answers; and the characteristics of the interviewers themselves. All these data can help us to grasp the extent and the causes of the various types of non-sampling error.

The analysis may serve to suggest more effective survey design. In fact, we have shown the lower response rate observed for wealthier households, which the usually employed stratification and post-stratification criteria are not able to correct properly. The availability of data on the average market value of houses by neighbourhood within the main cities suggests that serious consideration should be given to revising these criteria. Another solution might be the over-sampling of wealthier households to improve the efficiency of some overall estimators.

Specific techniques for collecting sensitive information are available. More generally, the questionnaire should be designed to include careful evaluation of various aspects of apparently less problematic questions as well.

Another matter for further research, on which work is under way, is interviewer effects: heterogeneous performances among interviewers in terms of response rate and measurement error. The results could help us to improve selection and training procedures.

---

[20] Another technique for this purpose is the *randomized response technique* proposed by Warner (1965). However, this procedure is too cumbersome for a multi-purpose survey like the SHIW.

The work also showed that the sample estimates for income and wealth are seriously affected by underreporting, in spite of the efforts to overcome respondents' distrust. This evidence suggested increasing the share of panel households, which was accordingly raised from 25 % in 1991 to 55 % in 2008. Panel households, in fact, are better motivated to give truthful responses. The average credibility score for the panel households is greater than for households interviewed for the first time (7.73 as against 7.44 in 2008). However, while it may improve response credibility, increasing the panel proportion may reduce the coverage of particular population segments (e.g. young households) and worsen sample selection due to unit non-response. The terms of this trade-off need to be carefully evaluated.

As survey data users, we are aware that knowledge of the types of non-sampling errors can greatly improve both the specification of the empirical model and the interpretation of the results. In conclusion, we urge that in using surveys data practitioners maintain a critical reserve concerning the possible non-sampling errors affecting this type of data.

Acknowledgments We would like to thank the three anonymous referees for their valuable comments and suggestions to improve the quality of the paper. The views expressed are those of the authors and do not necessarily reflect those of the Bank of Italy.

References

Banca d'Italia. (2010). Household Wealth in Italy in 2009. *Supplements to the Statistical Bulletin* (new series) (Vol. 67), Banca d'Italia.

Banca d'Italia. (2010). Italian household budgets in 2008. *Supplements to the Statistical Bulletin* (new series) (Vol. 8), Banca d'Italia.

Biancotti, C., D'Alessio, G., & Neri, A. (2008). Measurement error in the bank of italy's survey of household income and wealth. *Review of Income and Wealth, 54*, 466–493.

Biemer, P.P., & Lyberg, L. (2003). *Introduction to Survey Quality.* Wiley Series in Survey Methodology. Hoboken: Wiley.

Biemer, P. P., & Trewin, D. (1997) A review of measurement error effects on the analysis of survey data. In L. Lyberg, P. Biemer, M. Collins, E. de Leeuw, C. Dippo, N. Schwarz, & D. Trewin (Eds.), *Survey Measurement and Process Quality* (pp. 603–632). New York: Wiley-Interscience.

Blom, A. (2011). Measuring interviewer effects across countries and surveys (pp. 18–22). Paper presented at the *Fourth conference of the european survey research association*, Lausanne.

Cannari, L., & D'Alessio, G. (1990). Housing assets in the bank of Italy's survey of household income and wealth. In C. Dagum, M. Zenga, (Eds.), *Proceedings of Income and Wealth Distribution, Inequality and Poverty* (pp. 326–334). Berlin: Springer.

Cannari, L., & D'Alessio, G. (1993). Non reporting and under reporting behaviour in the bank of Italy's survey of household income and wealth. In *Bulletin of the International Statistics Institute 49th Session* (pp. 395–412). Firenze: International Statistical Institute.

Cannari, L., D'Alessio, G., Raimondi, G., & Rinaldi, A. (1990). Le attività finanziarie delle famiglie italiane. *Temi di Discussione* (Vol. 136), Banca d'Italia.

Cohen, J. (1960). A coefficient of agreement for nominal scales. *Educational and Psychological Measurement, 20*, 37–46.

CRESME. (2010). Il Mercato delle costruzioni al 2011. *Rapporto congiunturale e previsionale* (Vol. 18), CRESME, Roma.

D'Alessio, G., & Faiella, I. (2002) Nonresponse behaviour in the bank of Italy's survey of household income and wealth. *Temi di Discussione* (Vol. 462), Banca d'Italia.

D'Aurizio, L., Faiella, I., Iezzi, S., & Neri, A. (2006). L'underreporting della ricchezza finanziaria nell'indagine sui bilanci delle famiglie. *Temi di Discussione* (Vol. 610), Banca d'Italia.

De Luca, G., Peracchi, F. (2011). Estimating engel curves under unit and item nonresponse. *Journal of Applied Econometrics*. doi:10.1002/jae.1232

Groves, R. M., & Couper, M. P. (1998). *Nonresponse in Household Interview Surveys*. New York: Wiley.

Hand, D., Mannila, H., & Smyth, P. (2001). *Principles of Data Mining*. Cambridge: MIT Press.

Heckman, J. (1979). Sample selection bias as a specification error. *Econometrica, 47*, 153–161.

Heise, D. (1969). Separating reliability and stability in test-retest correlation. *American Sociological Review, 34*, 93–101.

Iannacchione, V. G. (2003). Sequential weight adjustments for location and cooperation propensity for the 1995 national survey of family growth. *Journal of Official Statistics, 19*, 31–43.

Kalton, G., & Flores Cervantes, I. (2003) Weighting methods. *Journal of Official Statistics, 19*, 81–97.

Krippendorff, K. (2004). Reliability in content analysis: some common misconceptions and recommendations. *Human Communication Research, 30*, 411–433.

Krippendorff, K. (2007). *Computing krippendorff's alpha reliability*. Departmental papers 43, Annenberg School for Communication, University of Pennsylvania.

Lessler, J., & Kalsbeek, W. (1992). *Nonsampling Error in Survey*. Wiley Series in Probability and Mathematical Statistics. New York: Wiley.

Little, R., & Rubin, D. (1987). *Statistical Analysis with Missing Data*. New York: Wiley.

Little, R., & Vartivarian, S. (2005). Does weighting for nonresponse increase the variance of survey means? *Survey Methodology, 31*, 161–168 (2005).

Lord, F., & Novick, M. (1968). *Statistical theories of mental test scores*. Reading: Addison-Wesley.

Neri, A., & Zizza, R. (2010). Income reporting behaviour in sample surveys. *Temi di Discussione* (Vol. 777), Banca d'Italia (2010).

Pissarides, C.A., & Weber, G. (1989). An expenditure-based estimate of Britain's black economy. *Journal of Public Economics, 39*, 17–32 (1989).

Raghavarao, D., & Federer, W. (1979). Block total response as an alternative to the randomized response method in surveys. *Journal of the Royal Statistical Society Series B, 41*, 40–45.

Särndal, C. E., & Lundström, S. (2005). *Estimation in Surveys with Nonresponse*. Wiley series in survey methodology, Chichester: Wiley.

Singh, A. C., & Mohl, C. A. (1996). Undertsanding calibration estimators in survey sampling. *Survey Methodology, 22*, 107–115.

Warner, S. L. (1965). Randomized-response: a survey technique for eliminating evasive answer bias. *Journal of the American Statistical Association, 60*, 63–69.

Part IV
Data Integration

Enriching a Large-Scale Survey from a Representative Sample by Data Fusion: Models and Validation

Tomàs Aluja-Banet, Josep Daunis-i-Estadella and Yan Hong Chen

Abstract Data Fusion is a series of operations which takes advantage of collected information. Here we present a complete, real practice of Data Fusion, focussing on all the necessary operational steps carried out. These steps define the actual key points of such a procedure: selection of the hinge variables, grafting donors and recipients, choosing the imputation model and assessing the quality of the imputed data. We present a standard methodology for calibrating the convenience of the chosen imputation model. To that end we use a validation suite of seven statistics that measure different facets of the quality of the imputed data: comparing the marginal global statistics, assessing the truthfulness of imputed values and evaluating the goodness of fit of the imputed data. To measure the adequacy of the recipient individuals in respect to the donor set, we compute the significance of the validation statistics by bootstrapping under the assumption that recipients are a random sample of the donor population. To illustrate the proposed approach, we perform a real data fusion operation on the victimization of citizens, where the collected imputation of opinion on perceived safety is used to enrich a large scale survey on citizen victimization.

T. Aluja-Banet (✉)
Universitat Politècnica de Catalunya—Barcelona Tech, Barcelona, Spain
e-mail: tomas.aluja@upc.edu

J. Daunis-i-Estadella
Universitat de Girona, Campus de Montilivi, Girona , Spain
e-mail: josep.daunis@udg.edu

Y. H. Chen
Institut d'Estadística de Catalunya, Barcelona, Spain
e-mail: yhong@idescat.cat

C. Davino and L. Fabbris (eds.), *Survey Data Collection and Integration*,
DOI: 10.1007/978-3-642-21308-3_8, © Springer-Verlag Berlin Heidelberg 2013

121

1 Introduction to Data Fusion

Data fusion, also known as statistical matching, is a technological operation whose aim is to integrate the information of two independent data sources. Technically it involves the imputation of a complete block of missing variables and is currently undertaken for specific entrepreneurial purposes (Rässler 2002; D'Orazio et al. 2006; Rubin 1987). Its main applications are in media surveys, where they are used to integrate two data sources, such as consumption and audience, into data collection. These are situations in which reducing the ever increasing burden caused by official statistics is a difficult problem to face, as well as fusing the web flow data with survey data.

Here, we address the problem in its simplest case, in which there are two files: the donor file with complete information $(X_0; Y_0)$, and the recipient file with just (X_1) variables. The X variables are currently called *common, link, hinge or bridge* variables, while the Y variables are the *specific, fusing or imputing* variables. The objective of the data fusion is to transfer the specific variables of the donor file to the recipient file at an individual level (this operation is called unilateral fusion).

This operation is common practice at statistical institutes, where it is used as a means for enriching a large survey with data from a small scale survey, i.e., a survey that includes some questions that are difficult to ask in the large survey.

We have applied this schema to delve into the perceived safety of citizens in Catalonia, where a large survey on victimization is held every year. We also account for the actual level of crimes and offences in the population, whether they be reported or not. This research has been conducted under the framework of the Catalan Institute of Statistics (IDESCAT) and the Universitat Politècnica de Catalunya agreement of 2007–2011, to develop methodologies for data fusion for enhancing the production of regional statistics. The goal is to enrich this information with opinions on perceived safety coming from an independent survey. Thus, the purpose of the data fusion operation is to relate the opinions on perceived safety with the more objective information on victimization.

It can be argued that having a single source combining both types of information would be the ideal situation; however, the cost entailed by such a large survey comprising all manner of questions, combined with the burden imposed on respondents, makes data fusion a feasible alternative for a better use of the available information. Data fusion does not create new information, but it increases its value simply by combining the available data. Hence, when the information is incomplete, data fusion is a conceivable technique for taking advantage of collected data.

It can be shown that this operation, though with a different global aim, is similar to that which preserves the confidentiality of respondents regarding sensitive information (Burridge 2003).

2 Conditions for Data Fusion

The aim of this paper is to focus on some key points that very often require valid data fusion:

Representative samples: Usually it is taken for granted that both files need to be random samples of the same population; but this is not the case in many data fusion operations. Imagine, for instance, that we are interested in fusing the characteristics of visitors to the webpage of a company with the actual clients of the company. In data fusion, we do not need to assume that both files are samples drawn independently from the same parent population. In fact, both files may not be any sample at all (Lebart and Lejeune 1995). Our aim is to complete the information of the recipient file, that is, to form a fused file $(X_1, \hat{Y}_1)$, in such a way that $\hat{Y}_1$ can be a realization of $f(Y|X_1)$. Since missingness is induced by design, it implies a missing completely at random (MCAR) or missing at random (MAR) scheme, depending on whether both files are random samples of the same distribution or not (Rubin 1987; Rässler 2004).

Predictive relevance. To obtain valid imputed data, we need to assume that the X variables account for all significant variability of the Y variables, given the imputation model; otherwise imputed values won't reveal the underlying phenomena that we are trying to reproduce. That is, $Y = i(X) + \varepsilon$, where $i(X) = \hat{Y}$ stands for the imputation model and ε just conveys random fluctuations. We call this assumption the "predictive relevance" of the common variables with respect to the specific ones. This assumption entails the usual conditional independence assumption $E[Y, Z|X] = 0$, for any other dataset Z.

Conditional imputation. Hence, to obtain valid imputed data, we need to impute conditionally to X variables (Rubin 1987). Clearly this is the only way to reproduce the multivariate distribution $f(X, Y)$ in the fused data file. This is, however, a very strict goal. In practice it can be argued that we just need to reproduce up to the second moments, $E[X, Y]$, since subsequent analyses usually only rely on the computation of covariance matrices.

Deterministic versus stochastic. If we perform a deterministic imputation (i.e. $i(X) = E[Y|X]$), imputed values would minimize the prediction error $E[Y_1 - \hat{Y}_1]^2$ (Aluja-Banet et al. 2007), but they would exhibit artificial regularity, which implies that variances of imputed values will underestimate the true variance of specific variables. What's more, the covariances that are computed from the imputed values $Cov(\hat{Y}_1)$ and $Cov(X_1, \hat{Y}_1)$ will overestimate the true covariances (Schafer 1999). However, it is useful to bear in mind that if prediction is the purpose of data fusion, a deterministic imputation is the best way to obtain individual estimates.

In general, the purpose of data fusion is to simulate a real instance (X, Y) of data. This implies that we need to perform stochastic imputation. That is, taking as imputed value a random draw of the conditional distribution, $i(X) \leftarrow f(Y|X)$.

Imputation needs to be stochastic in order to reproduce the current distribution of imputed data; that is, its variability, covariability and the joint distribution $f(X, Y)$.

We call matching noise the discrepancy between $f(X_1, Y_1)$ and $f(X_1, \hat{Y}_1)$ (Paass 1985; D'Orazio et al. 2006). Since the true joint distribution f of data is unknown, we are compelled to evaluate it empirically by comparing the empirical distributions $\hat{f}(X_1, Y_1)$, and $\hat{f}(X_1, \hat{Y}_1)$.

Single versus multiple imputation. Finally, imputed data are not like actual, observed data; it is an estimate, and hence it conveys random fluctuation. Rubin dealt with this problem in 1986 and proposed to embed the variability of imputed values into the fused data file. This is achieved by multiple imputation (Rubin 1987; Rässler 2004; Schafer 1999).

Multiple imputation improves the results of single imputation since it combines several possible imputations. Averaging the estimates, we obtain more accurate and more stable statistics than those obtained with a single (punctual) estimate (Aluja-Banet and Daunis-i-Estadella 2012).

3 Steps for a Data Fusion

To perform a data fusion operation we need to carry out the following steps:

1. Selection of the hinge variables.
2. Grafting recipients and donors in the same space.
3. Choosing the imputation model.
4. Assessing the quality of the imputed data.

3.1 Selection of the Hinge Variables

We call hinge variables the subset of the common variables that are present in both datasets: donors and recipients, which are selected as predictive variables in the imputation model. This is by far the most important step in any data fusion operation, since the validity of the operation lies in the aforementioned predictive relevance of the hinge. Of course, the selection of variables is bounded to the available common variables in the donor and recipient datasets.

The easiest possibility is to take a maximal available number of common variables in order to improve the predictive power of the common set. Nevertheless, this may not be the best option, since we may run into the curse of the dimensionality problem and into the instability of prediction due to the fact that non-informative and redundant predictors are included.

Thus, it is interesting to select a minimum subset of common variables with maximum predictive power among the specific ones, therefore defining the "hinge" of the fusion. We can achieve this by using standard multivariate statistical modeling techniques.

Since we are interested in defining a subset of X variables, by maximizing some predictive measure of $Y = f(X) + \varepsilon$, we use Redundance Analysis (a variant of

---

Algorithm

```
X <- X_0 r <- p
FOR k=1:(p-1)
    FOR j=1:r
        X <- X[,-j]
        COMPUTE RDA(X,Y_0)
        COMPUTE Tau by cross-validation
    ENDFOR
    k <- argmin Tau
    X <- X[,-k]
    r <- r-1
ENDFOR
PLOT(Tau)
```

Fig. 1 Algorithm for backward elimination of the most redundant variable

Canonical Correlation Analysis) (Rao 1964; Van Den Wollenberg 1977; Lauro and D'Ambra 1984), as a predictive measure of the relation between both sets of variables.

We obtain a minimal subset of the common X variables, by using a greedy backward algorithm, maximizing at each step

$$RDA(X, Y) = \sum_{\alpha=1}^{r} \sum_{j=1}^{q} cor^2(y_j, \psi_\alpha),\tag{1}$$

where ψ_α represents orthogonal components of X that are most correlated with the specific variables y_j; q is the number of specific variables and r is the dimensionality of the common space that equals $min(p, q)$, p being the number of common variables. If $p < q$, then Redundancy Analysis is equivalent to Principal Component Regression Analysis. The objective function is the sum of the squared correlation of the components of the X space with the specific variables.

This objective function finds components of the X space with optimal predictive power of the y_j variables. Hence, we can define an algorithm for backward elimination of the x_j variable that is most redundant with the remaining ones (Fig. 1). We evaluate the predictive power of the components by 10-fold cross-validation, as the ratio τ of the predicted error divided by the sum of squares of each variable:

$$\tau = \frac{\sum_j^q \sum_{i=1}^n (y_{ij} - \hat{y}_{ij})^2}{\sum_j^q \sum_{i=1}^n (y_{ij} - \bar{y}_j)^2}.\tag{2}$$

The lower the ratio, the more redundant is the variable to eliminate.

At each step, the most redundant common variable is eliminated. At the end, the τ values computed at each step are plotted; the minimum value identifies the subset of the common variables that are most predictive of the specific ones.

3.2 Grafting the Recipient in the Space of Donors

Grafting the recipient information into the donor space means positioning donors and recipients in the same factorial subspace. Once the hinge variables have been selected, it is worthwhile to see them visually in the same reference subspace defined by the hinge (both clouds of individuals and variables) in order to assess differences in the multivariate structure of either of the datasets. For that purpose, the user must declare the hinge variables of donors as an active set, whereas the specific variables and the recipients must be declared illustrative. Then, the common factorial subspace is easily obtained by a factorial descriptive analysis of the active table. Finally, the common space can be used to display all the information present in the donor and recipient files, providing a visual idea of whether or not both files are issued from the same population with the same multivariate structure. It also validates the predictive power of the hinge variables, vis-a-vis the specific variables (Rius 1999).

3.3 Choosing the Imputation Model

There are three basic imputation models for data fusion. The first one consists of embedding the common and specific variables within a *parametric* multivariate distribution $f(X, Y|\theta)$, assuming that donors and recipients are independently drawn at random from this distribution. It can be factored into $f(X, Y|\theta) = f(Y|X, \theta_{Y|X})f(X, \theta_X)$; thus, it is possible to estimate its parameters θ_X and $\theta_{Y|X}$ from the available information and use them to impute the missing block of data. The second approach consists of directly *modeling* the relationship between the Y variables and the X variables in the donor file by means of a regression function, $E(Y|X) = r(X)+\varepsilon$, and applying this model in the *recipient* file (*explicit modeling*). The last approach consists of finding for each individual of the recipient file one or more donor individuals that are as similar as possible, and then -in some way- transferring the values of the Y variables to the *recipient* individual (*implicit modeling*). This method is known as *hot deck*, a term borrowed from data editing.

The *parametric* imputation is bound to the missing data problem. It assumes a common distribution $f(X, Y|\theta)$ from which the donor and recipient file are random samples. Then, it maximizes the observed likelihood or, more commonly, uses the expectation maximization (EM) (Dempster et al. 1977) or data augmentation (DA) algorithm (Schaferand Olsen 1998). The EM algorithm is intended to estimate the parameters of the distribution without incorporating the variability of the estimated parameters, like the DA algorithm, which intends to simulate instances of the distributions by allowing variability of the parameters themselves. The EM or DA algorithm can be easily performed for a multinormal distribution in cases of continuous specific variables, or for a multinomial distribution in cases of categorical variables.

Explicit modeling can be performed by several methods, such as simultaneous multiple regression, principal component regression, partial least squares (PLS) regression, neural networks, multivariate adaptive regression splines, etc. It skips over the problem of formulating a parametric model, although it is easy to show that in the case of multivariate normality both approaches are equivalent.

Hot deck is the simplest method; it requires no assumption about the probabilistic distribution or about the formal relation between the specific and the common variables. It is a data-based method and, in this sense, it is distribution free. It can be a *random hot deck* when the donor (or donors) are selected at random within a specific group and these donors share some characteristics with the recipient; or it can be a *distance hot deck*, better known as the *knn* method, where the donor and recipients are placed in a common subspace defined by the common variables and then, for each recipient, its k-nearest donor neighbours are found and listed. Finally, the assignment is made based on this list. It is possible to mix both approaches, i.e., choosing by distance hot deck a list of neighbours which share some characteristics with the recipient individual. Hot deck methodology implies performing random draws from the empirical conditional distribution $\hat{f}(Y|X, \theta_{Y|X})$.

Depending on the imputation model, we will obtain some properties from the imputed data. In the comparisons performed on health data (Aluja-Banet and Daunis-i-Estadella 2012), Data Augmentation (DA) demonstrates a better capacity for preserving the multivariate distribution of imputed variables, their correlations among variables and their marginal statistics (means and variances). However, DA fails to reproduce the actual values of imputed variables and delivers poor results on the matching noise. On the other hand, methods based on the hot deck approach fail to preserve, as before, the multivariate structure and marginal statistics; but they deliver values as if they were real, with the best matching noise results. Regarding explicit modeling techniques, they place themselves in an intermediate position between the previous two approaches: they perform well in the accuracy and randomness of residuals of the imputed variables.

The hybrid alternative

As has been stated, the parametric and the non-parametric approaches show complementary properties; hence, it is natural to complement them in a hybrid approach so as to avoid nuisances and to benefit from the advantages of both. The hybrid approach has been proposed by Rässler (2002). It consist of performing a DA algorithm as a first step by imputing the $\hat{Y}_1$ values; then secondly, finding per each imputed recipient $(\hat{y}_{ij}^1, j = 1, ..., q)$ its closest donor (by $1nn$) and transferring its actual values on the specific variables to the recipient. This last step can only make the imputed values more real at the first stage, without causing too much damage to the good properties of the former values.

3.4 Validation Tools

As a final step of a data fusion operation, we need to validate the quality of the fused data. We need to calibrate it as an actual instance of $f(X, Y)$. This is not an obvious task. In practice, several suites of statistics have been proposed (Van Der Putten et al. 2002; Rässler 2004; Lebart and Lejeune 1995; Aluja-Banet et al. 2007); each one focussing on one facet of the validation process (quality is, as always, a multidimensional concept).

Here we will use a series of statistics. For the sake of simplicity, they consist of just averaging the univariate comparison tests of the fused data set $(X_1, \hat{Y}_1)$ with the observed data (X_0, Y_0), since testing multivariate parametric hypothesis becomes unrealistic when the problem grows in complexity.

In practice, however, we need to differentiate the ideal validation, where the comparison would be made with the true data on recipients (X_1, Y_1) rather than the true data on donors (X_0, Y_0). Clearly the former can only be made in planned experiments for assessing the quality of a validation methodology; since in general we won't have the specific variables for recipients Y_1 (otherwise the imputation won't make sense). Validation with respect to the donors results in an optimistic view of the validation, since the matching noise corresponding to the mismatch between donors and recipients is lost; however, it can permit discernment of the optimal imputation method for a given data fusion operation and its outstanding properties.

To assess the value of the fusion, we have split the validation stage into seven points, going from the most trivial to the most demanding.

3.4.1 Comparison of Marginal Statistics

The first thing to assess is the coherence of the marginal statistics in both files (means, variances and frequencies in the case of categorical variables), in respect to the common and the specific variables. This is pertinent regardless of whether or not it is appropriate to assume that the random samples of donors and recipients come from the same population. These comparisons arise from several tests (t-test, F, χ^2...), one for each variable with its corresponding p-value. We summarize them in one statistic called the *Average Significance Level* (*ASL*), defined as an average p-value (*ASLm* for the mean, *ASLs* for the standard deviations and *ASLf* for the frequencies):

$$ASL = 1 - \left(\prod_{i=1}^{r} (1 - \alpha_i) \right)^{1/r}, \tag{3}$$

where r is the number of univariate tests performed and α_i their corresponding p-value.

This comparison, when made upon the common variables (X_0, X_1), may confirm that both samples are representative of the same population; when made upon the specific variables $(Y_1, \hat{Y}_1)$, it may assess the unbiasness of the imputation.

3.4.2 Comparison of the Internal Coherence of Imputed Values

Secondly, we want to test the difference between the pairwise correlations among the imputed specific variables on recipients and those observed in donors. We summarize them in one statistic defined as the mean absolute difference of correlations computed between the specific variables in the observed data Y_0 and in the fused data $\hat{Y}_1$. We call this statistic the *Average Correlation Difference of the internal coherence, ACD_{int}* of the fused data.

We use the Pearson correlation to compare the correlations between continuous variables and the correlation of the optimal quantifications (Greenacre 1984), if we deal with categorical variables.

$$ACD_{int} = \frac{\sum_{j,j'} |cor(y_j^0, y_{j'}^0) - cor(\hat{y}_j^1, \hat{y}_{j'}^1)|}{s}, \tag{4}$$

where y^0 and $\hat{y}^1$ refer to the observed specific variables in the donor file and the imputed specific variables in the fused data file respectively, whereas s is the total number of pairs of specific variables (j, j').

3.4.3 Comparison of the External Coherence of Imputed Values

Preserving the pairwise correlations between the specific variables is not enough to assure the quality of the imputed data. For instance, complete random hot deck can assure internal coherence but will be completely uncorrelated with the common variables. To obtain valid imputed data, it is necessary to preserve the correlation between specific and common variables. Consequently, we compute the average absolute difference of pairwise correlations between the specific variables and the external variables computed in the donor file and in the recipient file. We call this statistic *ACD of the external coherence (ACD_{ext})*, and it can be applied to any available variable except for the specific ones. As before, we compute the Pearson correlation coefficient for the continuous variables, the correlation of optimal quantification for the categorical ones and the correlation ratio for the mixed case (Saporta 2006). It is useful to assess whether we are reproducing the correlation matrix $cor(X, Y)$ in the recipient R.

$$ACD_{ext} = \frac{\sum_{j,j'} |cor(y_j^0, x_{j'}^0) - cor(\hat{y}_j^1, x_{j'}^1)|}{t}, \tag{5}$$

where t is the number of pairs of variables: one is common and the other specific.

3.4.4 Comparison of the Second-Order Moments

Depending on the subsequent data analysis, many data fusion operations need only to preserve the second-order moments. We can assess this by computing the weighted correlation (wc), of the eigenvectors of the correlation matrix of the observed data $cor(Y_0)$, with the eigenvectors of the correlation matrix of the imputed data $cor(\hat{Y}_1)$, where the weight equals the corresponding eigenvalue (Rius 1999).

$$wc = \frac{\sum_\alpha^A \lambda_\alpha \left| u'_{Y_0\alpha} . u_{\hat{Y}_1\alpha} \right|}{\sum_\alpha^a \lambda_\alpha},$$ (6)

where A is the number of significant factorial components of Y_0, λ_α is the α-th eigenvalue and $u_{Y_0\alpha}$ its corresponding eigenvector.

3.4.5 Evaluating the Matching Noise

Another desirable property of imputed variables is the reproduction in the recipients of the true probability distribution $f(X, Y)$. Since the true distribution function is unknown, we content ourselves to compare the empirical distribution function of recipients in respect to the empirical distribution function of donors. In order to assess the matching noise, we compute the Smirnov distance between every pair of fused and observed variables (Conti et al. 2006) and the difference between the empirical distribution of each observed variable y_j with their corresponding imputed one y_j. We do so for each specific variable and, finally, we average the results. We call the resulting statistic the *Average Smirnov Distance* (ASD):

$$ASD = \frac{\sum_j sd_j}{q}$$ (7)

where sd_j stands for the Smirnov distance calculated for the specific variable j, and q is the number of specific variables. We can compute the significance of this average Smirnov distance (ASD) to get an idea about the magnitude of the matching noise (Lebart et al. 1984).

3.4.6 Computing the Individual Prediction Error

The prediction error would be the first statistic which a statistician would be interested in; but in general it is not relevant in a data fusion operation, since optimizing the prediction error implies worsening the randomness of data and, hence, moving away from the $f(X, Y)$. However, in some applications, this characteristic is the one of interest. We compute it by comparing the imputed individual values with the observed ones; we relativize this error in respect to the error that would be obtained if we were to impute the mean for a continuous variable or the mode for a categorical variable. Finally we average this ratio for all the specific variables (Y_1).

$$\tau = \frac{1}{q} \sum_{j}^{q} \frac{\sum_{i}^{n_1} (y_{ij}^1 - \hat{y}_{ij}^1)^2}{\sum_{i}^{n_1} (y_{ij}^1 - \bar{y}_{j}^1)^2} \tag{8}$$

The ratio allows us to assess the accuracy of the imputed values. A value greater than 1 indicates a prediction error worse than imputing by the default value.

3.4.7 Randomness of Residuals

The last statistic consists of testing the assumption of the predictive relevance of the hinge variables in respect to the fusing variables. Under this hypothesis the residuals $\varepsilon = Y_0 - \hat{Y}_0$ should convey just random fluctuation. We assume that residuals follow a multivariate normal distribution with a zero mean vector and unknown covariance matrix Σ. Then, we wish to test the hypothesis of sphericity, namely $H_0 : \Sigma = \sigma^2 I_q$, where $\sigma^2 > 0$ is an unknown positive constant.

For the sake of interpretability, we just compute the ratio between the arithmetic and geometric means of the eigenvectors λ_j of the correlation matrix of the residuals $cor(\varepsilon) = cor(Y_0 - \hat{Y}_0)$:

$$Rnd\,Res = \frac{\frac{1}{q} \sum_{j=1}^{q} \lambda_j}{\sqrt[q]{\prod_{j=1}^{q} \lambda_j}} \tag{9}$$

In summary, these statistics provide an overall evaluation of the quality of imputed data, focussing on the different aspects once data fusion has been performed. Of course, comparing $\hat{Y}_1$ with the actual values of Y_1 would be more relevant than if we impute the donors and compare $\hat{Y}_0$ with Y_0, in order to have a precise evaluation of the quality of imputed values; but in a normal situation we don't have the Y_1 values.

As a general rule, we can group these statistics, depending on the aspect of the fused data that they measure, as follows. The desirable value for each statistic is provided:

Statistics comparing the marginal global statistics

- *ASLm* and *ASLs* values as high as possible (they are averages of *p-values*).

Statistics assessing the multivariate distribution of data

- *ACDi* and *ACDe* as low as possible, since they are differences in correlations.
- *wc* giving an overall correlation of the multivariate distributions, so a value close to one is the target.

Statistic assessing the truthfulness of imputed values

- *ASD* measuring the distance with the empirical cumulative distribution; thus, the lower the values the better the imputation,

Statistics evaluating the goodness of the imputed data

- τ measuring the relative prediction error; hence, low values are desired, and
- *RndRes*, ratio of the arithmetic mean of residual eigenvalues to their geometric mean; hence, values close to one are the target.

4 Significance of the Validation Statistics

After having performed a data fusion operation, we can always compute the suite of the validation statistics. Then, the issue is how much they are significant or whether they attain normal values or not. We can clear it up by building their sampling distribution under the assumption that recipients are a random sample of the donor population. We achieve this by bootstrapping the donor file X_0, drawing random samples from the donor file with size n_1 (the recipient size), then computing for each bootstrap sample the corresponding validation statistics.

From the set of bootstrap values of each statistic, we can build their density distribution. Then, for a given value of every statistic computed in the actual performed data fusion, we can compute the corresponding *p-value*.

P-values are computed as the probability of having a statistic with a value equal to or larger than the one obtained, according to the sense of the alternative hypothesis per each one. For example, the *p-value* for the *ASLm* statistic is the area on the left of the observed statistic, since lower values of the *ASLm* would imply that the marginal statistics in the compared files are different; whereas the *p-value* for the *ACDi* will be computed on the right of the observed statistic, since values greater than the observed value would imply that correlations between variables in both datasets are more different than the existing correlations with the observed value. A *p-value* lower than a prefixed threshold would reveal that recipients behave differently from what is expected from donors when regarding the considered statistic.

5 Application to Official Statistics

Over the last few years, surveys on safety and victimization have spread throughout many countries, and they commonly serve as a complement to police and judicial statistics. In Catalonia, IDESCAT (Statistical Institute of Catalonia) annually conducts such a survey. The underlying hypothesis is that the socioeconomic characteristics and the experienced victimization preclude opinions regarding the proximal perception of citizens' safety.

Our purpose is to impute the opinions on perceived safety collected from surveys on citizen victimization. Hence, the opinions on safety are the specific set of variables to be imputed; whereas the socioeconomic characteristics and victimization questions, present in both datasets, are the common variables.

Fig. 2 Factorial map
of donors (*black dots*) and
recipients (*grey dots*)

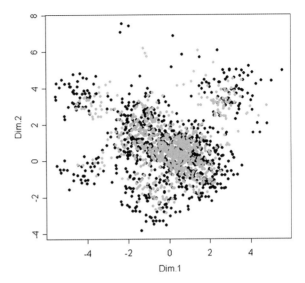

To that end, we use data collected in 2006 on victimization and the perceived safety of citizens in order to impute their opinions in the 2007 victimization survey. The set of imputed questions pertained to: level of safety in the neighborhood and in the city; global appreciation of municipal police services; problems with home, immigration, crime and community spirit. Hence, the 2006 survey constitutes the donor file whereas the 2007 file constitutes the recipient file.

Fortunately, the specific variables were also present in the 2007 survey; thus, we have the actual 2007 values of the specific variables to validate the imputed opinion values from the 2006 survey.

We have 11030 donors coming from the 2006 survey and 7410 recipients coming from the 2007 survey. The specific variables, although measured on an ordinal scale and not following a normal distribution, were treated as if they were continuous.

As a first step, we have selected the hinge variables by the greedy procedure described in Sect. 3.1, ending up with 10 components with maximum predictive power of the specific variables.

In Fig. 2, we give the positioning of donors and recipients in the same common space of the hinge variables. We can see that both sets form two homogeneous distributions with no significant difference between them. This is because both data files are representative samples of the same population.

We have used a hybrid imputation model for our imputation model. In this way, we retain the most favourable properties of both parametric modeling and the *Inn* model. Hence, we have used a parametric imputation method by Data Augmentation, performing Multiple Imputation (*MI*) 10 times to cope with the variability of the imputed data. Then, for each single imputed data set we have performed *Inn* imputations of the specific variables to obtain an imputed data set of realistic values.

Table 1 Validation statistics of the proposed data fusion

	ASLm	ASLs	ACDi	ACDe	Tau	wc	ASD	RndRes
Y_1	0.0060	1.03e-06	0.0337	0.0268	1.7640	0.9921	0.0904	1.1778

Table 2 Percentiles of the validation statistics of our data fusion

	ASLm	ASLs	ACDi	ACDe	Tau	wc	ASD	RndRes
Percentile	0.139	0.074	0.227	1.000	1.000	0.309	0	0.771

Finally, we have computed the validation statistics of the multiple imputed data $\hat{Y}_1$ with the actual observed Y_1 on recipients (since we have this information). The synthetic validation statistics are given in Table 1.

Then, to assess the significance of these statistics we have performed 400 bootstrap samples. In Fig. 3 we represent the density functions of the 8 validation statistics obtained from the 400 bootstrap resamples. For each statistic, we display the density obtained from the bootstrap and a vertical line represents the actual statistic obtained by our data.

Then, from the actual computed value and the desirable values specified in Sect. 3, we can compute the significance of each statistic. The corresponding *p-value*, according to the densities obtained by bootstrap resampling to each validation statistic, is given in Table 2.

According to the results obtained, we can validate the performed data fusion. The global means obtained in $\hat{Y}_1$ are not very different from those actually observed in Y_1 (*p-value* of 0.139), whereas a larger discrepancy exists regarding the global variability of imputed variables (*p-value* of 0.074).

The correlations among the specific variables are fairly well reproduced (*p-value* of 0.227), but the correlations of the specific variables with the hinge variables are very well reproduced, much better from what we could expect when imputing a random set of donors (*p-value* of 1.000).

The overall weighted correlation, comparing the multivariate structure of Y_1 with the multivariate structure of $\hat{Y}_1$ is also fairly reproduced (*p-value* of 0.309).

The prediction error (Tau statistic) and the randomness of residuals (*RndRes* statistic) deliver good results (*p-values* of 1.00 and 0.771 respectively), indicating that the imputed values are much closer to the true ones than we could expect when imputing from a random sample of donors.

And finally, the Average Smirnov Distance has a *p-value* of 0, indicating in this case, that, in spite of the *1nn* correction performed, the imputed empirical distributions of variables are far from what we could obtain if we impute from a random sample of donors.

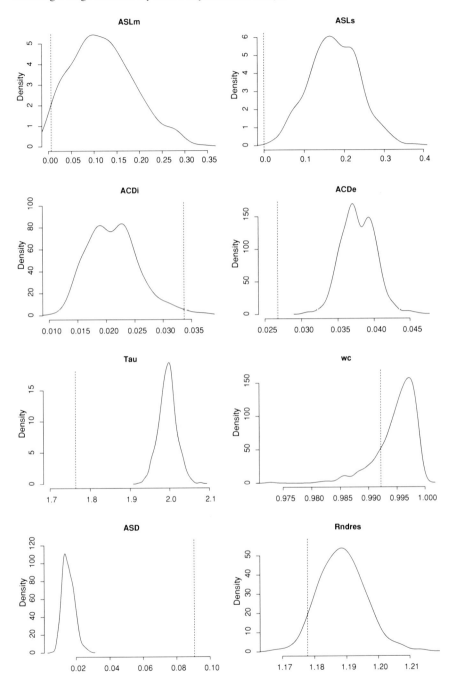

Fig. 3 Densities of validation statistics obtained in 400 bootstrap samples. *Vertical line* corresponds to our data fusion validation statistic

6 Conclusions

Data Fusion is a series of operations that takes advantage of available collected information that, with some cautions, allow us to obtain an instance of the recipient data by incorporating the uncertainty of imputation with data that can be used for subsequent analysis. In this paper, we have presented the conditions to be taken into account when performing such operations, the different imputation model, the hybrid alternative which combines the advantages of the parametric and non-parametric imputation model and the suite of validation statistics. These validation statistics are very synthetic and simple. They focus on one facet of the comparison, since multivariate tests are too restrictive and unrealistic in data fusion operations.

Finally, a procedure to assess the significance of these statistics is presented by using bootstrap on the donors. The reference distribution of the statistics under the null hypothesis can be easily computed on the recipients being a random sample of donors. From this, it is possible to have a critical view of the actual values of the validation statistics in respect to those obtained from a random sample of donors.

The possibility of adapting the random sample of donors to the actual design that is present in the recipient dataset would make the procedure more flexible and the comparisons more meaningful .

References

Aluja-Banet, T., & Daunis-i-Estadella, J. (2012): Validation and uncertainty in data fusion (submitted 2012).

Aluja-Banet, T., Daunis-i-Estadella, J., & Pellicer, D.: GRAFT, a complete system for data fusion. *Journal of Computational Statistics and Data Analysis, 52*(2), 635–649.

Bethel, J. (1989). Sample allocation in multivariate surveys. *Survey Methodology, 15*, 46–57.

Burridge, J. (2003) Information preserving statistical obfuscation. *Statistics and Computing, 13*, 321–327.

Conti, P. L., Marella, D Scanu, M. (2006). Nonparametric evaluation of matching noise. In: A. Rizzi, M. Vichi (Eds.), *Compstat 2006–Proceedings in Computational Statistics* (pp. 453–460). Heidelberg: Physica-Verlag.

Dempster, A. P., Laird, N. M., & Rubin, D. B. (1977). Maximum likelihood from incomplete data via the EM algorithm. *Journal of the Royal Statistical Society, B 39*, 1–38.

D'Orazio, M., Di Zio, M., & Scanu, M. (2006) *Statistical Matching: Theory and Practice*. Chichester: Wiley.

Greenacre, M. J. (1984). *Theory and Applications of Correspondence Analysis*. London: London Academic Press.

Lauro, C., & D'Ambra, L. (1984). L'analyse non symmetrique des correspondances (Non-symmetrical correspondence analysis). In: E. Diday (Ed.) *Data Analysis and Informatics-III* (p. 446). Amsterdam: Elsevier.

Lebart, L., & Lejeune, M. (1995). Assessment of data fusions and injections. In: *Encuentro Internacional AIMC sobre Investigación de Medios* (pp. 208–225).

Lebart, L., Morineau, A., & Warwick, K. M. (1984). *Multivariate Descriptive Statistical Analysis*. New York: Wiley.

Paass, G. (1985). Statistical record linkage methodology, state of the art and future prospects. Bulletin of the International Statistical Institute, In: *Proceedings of 45th Session*, LI, Book 2.

Rässler, S. (2002). *Statistical Matching: A Frequentist Theory Practical Applications and Alternative Bayesian Approaches*. New York: Springer.

Rässler, S. (2004). Data fusion: identification problems, validity and multiple imputation. *Austrian Journal of Statistics*, *33*(1&2), 153–171.

Rao, C. R. (1964). The use and interpretation of principal component analysis in applied research. *Sankhyā: The Indian Journal of Statistics, Series A*, *26*(4), 329–358.

Rius, R., Aluja, T., & Nonell, R. (1999). File grafting in market research. *Applied Stochastic Models in Business and Industry*, *15*(4), 451–460.

Rubin, D. B. (1987). *Multiple Imputation for Nonresponse in Surveys*. New York: Wiley.

Saporta, G. (2006). *Probabilités, Analyse des Données et Statistique*. Paris: Editions Technip.

Schafer, J. (1999). Multiple imputation: a primer. *Statistical Methods in Medical Research*, *8*(1), 3–15 (1999)

Schafer, J., & Olsen, M. K. (1998). Multiple imputation for multivariate missing-data problems: a data analyst's perspective. *Multivariate Behavioral Research*, *33*, 545–571.

Van Den Wollenberg, A. L. (1977). Redundancy analysis. An alternative for canonical correlation analysis. *Psychometrika*, *42*(2), 207–219.

Van Der Putten, P., Kok, J. N., & Gupta, A. (2002). *Data Fusion through Statistical Matching*. Technical Report MIT Sloan Working Paper, 4342-02, Eller College Working Paper No. 1031-05.

A Business Survey on Job Vacancies: Integration with Other Sources and Calibration

Diego Bellisai, Stefania Fivizzani and Marina Sorrentino

Abstract Statistical sources on the demand side of the labour market have been historically developed later than those on the supply side. A quarterly business survey was set up by ISTAT in 2003 to contribute to fill in some of these gaps, in particular, those on job vacancies and hours worked. Attention has been paid, when designing the survey and especially for the processing procedures, to the already existing sources, in order to fully exploit the available information in the editing and imputation and grossing up phases, and to ensure consistency among aggregate data produced by different sources. In this paper, it is discussed how the integration between the data collected by the job vacancy and hours worked and two other Istat business surveys has shaped the data processing methods which are used to produce the quarterly job vacancy indicators and differentiated them from others used in short-term business statistics.

1 Introduction

Statistical sources on the demand side of the labour market have been developed historically later than those on the supply side. A quarterly business survey was set up by ISTAT in 2003 to contribute to fill in some of these gaps, in particular, those on job vacancies and hours worked. Attention has been paid, when designing the survey and especially the data processing procedures, to the already existing sources, in order to fully exploit the available information in the editing and imputation and

D. Bellisai (✉) · S. Fivizzani · M. Sorrentino
Istat, Rome, Italy
e-mail: bellisai@istat.it

S. Fivizzani
e-mail: fivizzan@istat.it

M. Sorrentino
e-mail: mrsorren@istat.it

C. Davino and L. Fabbris (eds.), *Survey Data Collection and Integration*,
DOI: 10.1007/978-3-642-21308-3_9, © Springer-Verlag Berlin Heidelberg 2013

grossing up phases, and to ensure consistency among aggregate data produced by different sources.

In this paper, after a description of the main characteristics of the survey (Sect. 2), it is discussed how the data processing methods have been designed in order to pursue these aims. In Sect. 3 the data editing and imputation processes are analysed, while in Sect. 4 the calibration procedure is described. Some concluding remarks and considerations on future developments can be found in Sect. 5.

2 Main Characteristics of the Job Vacancy Survey

A need for infra-annual information on job vacancies has emerged in recent years within the framework of the labour market short-term statistics.

A job vacancy is a paid post which can be newly created, unoccupied or about to become vacant, for which the employer is taking active steps and is prepared to take further steps to find a suitable candidate from outside his or her enterprise.

The importance of quarterly job vacancies indicators is emphasized at the European level by an EU regulation[1] and their inclusion in the Principal European Economic Indicators (PEEIs) on the labour market. Italy produces quarterly data on the job vacancy rate (that is the percentage ratio between job vacancies and the sum of vacancies and jobs) via the ISTAT survey on job vacancies and hours worked (in the following, VELA) since the third quarter 2003.

The main variables collected by VELA are: job vacancies on the last day of the reference quarter; jobs on the last day of the previous and reference quarter; hires and separations; hours worked as normal time and overtime, hours not worked but paid by the employer and wage supplementary fund hours in the quarter. All variables are measured separately for manual and non-manual workers (managers excluded). The main target parameters of the survey are: job vacancy rate, number of job vacancies, share of firms with vacancies, per capita hours worked, share of overtime over hours worked, ratio between hours of wage supplementation fund and hours worked. In the following, we will focus on the job vacancy rate.

The target population of the survey comprises all enterprises with at least 10 employees, classified in the NACE (Nomenclature statistique des activités économiques dans la Communauté européenne, or Statistical Classification of Economic Activities in the European Community) Rev. 2 sections B-N (industry and services sectors, excluding personal and social ones). The study unit is the enterprise.

As a frame for designing and drawing the sample, the most recent of the annual releases of the Italian Statistical Business Register (in the following, SBR) available at the beginning of each calendar year is used. In the 2009 release, the SBR included around 179,000 active firms of the considered sizes and economic activi-

---

[1] Regulation (EC) No 453/2008 of the European Parliament and of the Council, completed by two Commission Regulations, No 1062/2008 and 19/2009.

ties. The sample size is set, on the basis of data quality and costs considerations, at around 15,000 firms. All the enterprises with at least 500 employees in the frame are included in the sample; they were around 1,500 in the 2009 SBR. Furthermore, a stratified random sample of around 13,500 firms with 10–499 employees is drawn from the SBR using economic activity, firm size and geographical area as stratification variables. For what concerns economic activity, the classes on which the strata are defined are set on the basis of the study domains (the NACE divisions for sections B to E and G, and the NACE sections F and from H to N). For what concerns firm size, the stratification classes (10–19, 20–99, 100–499 employees) are based on considerations related to the number of units in the population. For what concerns geographical area, three classes are used (North, Centre and South). A first set of possible strata is obtained by considering jointly the classes defined for the three stratification variables. Those among the possible strata which include too few firms in the frame population are collapsed with neighbouring ones. In the end, 177 strata of firms with 10–499 employees are considered. At the beginning of each year, in preparation for the survey wave for the first quarter, the sample is renewed, using the newly available latest annual SBR release. The list of firms with 500 employees is updated on the basis of the new SBR. Furthermore, the firms with 10–499 employees which have already been in the sample for three years are substituted by an equal number of newly drawn ones.

For the 10–499 employee part, the sample allocation is carried out through the Bethel method (Bethel 1989), that is a constrained optimisation (where the sample size is minimised under constraints on the maximum values of the expected coefficients of variation for the interest variables in the study domains). In particular, the implementation of this method in the ISTAT generalized software MAUSS is used.[2]

Many other countries in Europe use similar survey designs for their job vacancy surveys. In particular, most countries use stratified random sampling, with economic activity, size and, in some cases, also geographical area as stratification variables.Furthermore, in many countries the study units above a given size threshold are completely enumerated.[3]

The target parameters are disseminated, in general, for the NACE Rev. 2 sections. Job vacancy rates have been published nationally since June 2010 via quarterly press releases and are available at the online databases I.stat (http://dati.istat.it) and ConIstat (http://con.istat.it/). Furthermore, they are used by Eurostat to calculate the European aggregates and are available on its website (http://ec.europa.eu/eurostat).

Data are collected mainly via CATI (Computer Assisted Telephone Interviewing) and/or Web, although a small share of questionnaires, usually registered by the CATI operators, are transmitted via fax or email. In particular, the first time an enterprise is included in the sample, it is requested to respond via telephone interviewing,

---

[2] See Di Giuseppe et al. (2004) for a description of the software and its methodological basis.

[3] The job vacancy survey methodologies have been described by the large majority of EU countries on the basis of a common template for the 1st International Workshop on Methodologies for Job Vacancy Statistics, held in Nuremberg in December 2008 (see http://circa.europa.eu/Members/irc/dsis/jobvacancy/library).

while afterwards it can opt for the web mode. Hence, the mix of data collection techniques varies from quarter to quarter in relation to the distance from the last sample rotation.On average, in 2010, 80 % of the respondents have been interviewed through CATI (or have sent a fax or email response which has been registered by the CATI operators), while the remaining 20 % used the Web mode.

The job vacancy variable has some characteristics which distinguish it from most other variables included in business surveys, and which could make it difficult to measure. Moreover, there is no auxiliary source, either a survey or an administrative one, that provides information on variables similar to job vacancies and which could be used in the assessment of the collected data. However, the survey operations bring about a lot of information on the difficulties that enterprises meet when answering questions on job vacancies. Particularly useful to this purpose are: the meetings with the CATI interviewers aimed at debriefing the data collection phase and the direct communication between survey experts and sampled enterprises.

The first source of difficulty in measuring job vacancies is related to the fact that their number is normally not recorded in the enterprise information system, unlike the number of jobs or other labour input variables, such as hours paid.

Moreover, some enterprises (in particular smaller ones) may miss to identify actions they perform as active search of candidates because, for example, most of the search activity is carried out by word of mouth via inquiries among their employees. Other enterprises, for example seasonal ones (such as hotels and restaurants in touristic areas), report that part of the people hired during the seasonal peaks come from a pool of persons who have worked for the same enterprises in previous years and have been re-contacted. In these circumstances, some firms fail to consider these positions as vacancies.

On the other hand, medium-sized and large enterprises search for candidates via more formal channels (for example, by contacting specialized "headhunting" agencies or advertising vacancies in the media) and sustain specific costs for this activity. Therefore, these enterprises could have less difficulties in measuring the number of job vacancies. Nonetheless also large firms can find problems in interpreting the questions and collecting information on the variable. For example, some of them constantly receive job inquiries and curricula from people in search of a job and they may not be able to recognise that reviewing the curricula with the intention of hiring candidates for specific positions gives rise to job vacancies.

Other enterprises, such as banks or large scale distribution retail trades, are organized in a large number of local units and face problems related to the level at which the decisions on hires are taken. Normally, the head office (to which the VELA questionnaire is addressed) determines how many people to hire and for which positions to activate search steps but, in some cases, this responsibility can be delegated to local units and the head office can be unable to timely collect the information from all of them.

3 Editing and Imputation

One of the guiding criteria in the editing and imputation phase of the VELA survey is represented by the integration with other two ISTAT surveys, the monthly survey on employment, hours worked, wages and labour cost in the large enterprises (henceforth Large Enterprises Survey, LES) and the administrative based survey on employment, wages and social contributions (henceforth OROS).

The principles underlying this operation and their implementation consist, on the one hand, in maximising the consistency of the indicators produced by the three surveys and, on the other hand, in fully exploiting the features of the surveys.

In order to better understand the process, we think it is useful to briefly describe the LES and OROS surveys.

LES collects monthly data from a panel of about 1,160 firms (which had an average of at least 500 employees in the base year 2005 and are classified in the B-N sections of the NACE Rev. 2 classification) the number of jobs at the end of the month, hires and separations, hours worked (with the same definitions as VELA) as well as variables related to wages and labour cost. OROS relies on the whole population of the DM10 (Dichiarazione Mensile) forms (now E-Mens) which all firms are due to monthly fill in and transmit to the National Institute for Social Security (INPS), in order to declare the compulsory social contributions. By integrating the information contained in these forms with that collected by LES for the panel firms, OROS produces quarterly indicators on wages, labour cost and jobs for the B-N sections of the NACE Rev. 2 classification.

The OROS survey measures jobs through the average, on the three months of the reference quarter, of the number of employees to whom at least one hour of work has been paid in each month, while VELA and LES measure the number of jobs at the beginning and at the end of the reference quarter (or month).

The information collected by LES and OROS is used in many phases of the data editing and imputation procedures:

1. For all the LES firms:

   - for both responding and non-responding units, jobs, hires and separations are imputed by substituting the data collected by VELA with data collected by LES;
   - for non-responding units, some of the variables collected by LES are used as matching variables for job vacancy rate imputation[4];

2. For the responding units not belonging to the LES panel:

---

[4] In the VELA survey the sample, and hence also the list of firms with at least 500 employees included in it, is updated annually, on the basis of the most recent annual release of the SBR. This ensures that this part of the population (as represented in the frame) is completely included in the VELA sample. When designing the sample the LES firms which have less than 500 employees in the most recent SBR release are treated as all the other frame units below this size threshold. However, in the editing and imputation and grossing up phases they are treated as all the other LES units.

- at the single unit level, OROS jobs are used as one of the auxiliary indicators for outlier identification and for grossing up VELA data;
- at the aggregate level, OROS jobs are used as auxiliary variable in the grossing up via calibration.

We would like to briefly clarify the way OROS jobs are used for outlier identification in the job variable for non-LES units responding to VELA. The definition of job used in the two surveys differs. First, in the VELA survey the average number of jobs is obtained as the average between the number of jobs at the beginning and at the end of the quarter, while in the OROS survey such average is obtained by averaging the three monthly jobs figures declared in the DM10 form. Second, the number of jobs in the DM10 form consists in all the job positions which have been active even for only one hour in the reference month. Therefore, the average number of jobs as measured by the surveys can be different, both because of measurement errors and of differences in the definition. However, since most of the differences due to the definition depend on the job turnover and since this variable is measured by VELA (through hires and separations), it is possible to take it into account in evaluating the discrepancies in the microdata of the two surveys. The analysis of the differences between average number of jobs measured by VELA and OROS for the same unit is carried out through a variant of the resistant fences method (Thompson and Sigman 1996).[5]

The integration among surveys produces consistency in the aggregate data. In particular, the estimates produced by VELA for the number of jobs by section are consistent with those by OROS regarding firms with at least 10 employees in each quarter. Moreover if we consider only the LES firms, the procedures adopted ensure that the estimates produced by VELA for the number of jobs at the end of a given quarter coincide with those that can be produced by the LES survey for the last month of that quarter.

3.1 Job Vacancies: Peculiarities, Implications and Editing and Imputation Methods

As it has been mentioned before, the job vacancy variable presents some features which distinguish it from many other variables which are usually collected in business surveys. First of all it can be difficult to collect, since it refers to a phenomenon which often is not recorded in the firms' information system (differently from what

---

[5] The resistant fences method is an approach for outlier detection which is outlier-resistant. It is based on sample quartiles. Let q_1 be the first quartile, q_3 the third quartile, and $H = q_3 - q_1$, the interquartile range. The standard resistant fences rules define outliers as ratios less than $q_1 - k \cdot H$ or greater than $q_3 + k \cdot H$, where k is a constant, which is usually set between 1.5 (inner fence) and 3 (outer fence). In our case, for some particular economic activities, we have set the constant to values larger than or equal to 4, to cope with sample distributions with very narrow interquartile ranges.

Fig. 1 Job vacancy distribution in the third quarter 2010

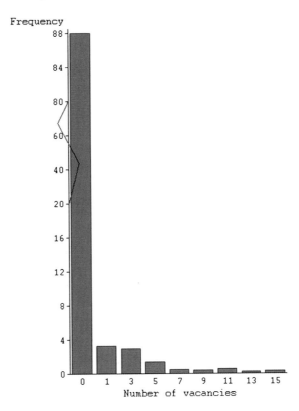

happens for employment and hours worked which are recorded for fiscal reasons) or is recorded in a rather informal way. This implies that even the date when the job search started can be difficult to reconstruct.

From an empirical point of view the distribution of the job vacancy variable is sharply concentrated on the zero value. Figure 1, which represents the job vacancy distribution for the third quarter 2010, shows that the share of firms which state not to have any job vacancies is slightly lower than 85%, while the share of firms with more than 10 vacancies is only about 1%.

Another important and problematic feature of the job vacancy variable is represented by its weak empirical relationship with other variables collected by the survey or obtainable from other sources. Exceptions are the relationships between job vacancy indicators and the firm size. In Table 1, it can be observed that, if all the survey respondents are considered, not only the average number of job vacancies per respondent but also the share of firms with vacancies are bigger for larger firms. However, if all the respondents are considered, the job vacancy rate has no clear relation with firm size. Nevertheless, if only the respondents with vacancies are considered, the job vacancy rate is found to be decreasing when size increases (and the average number of vacancies remains increasing with size also in this subset of respondents).

Table 1 Relationship between job vacancies and firm size (defined in terms of number of employees)—third quarter 2010

Firm size(employees)	Average number of job vacancies in all firms	Share of firms with job vacancies (%)	Job vacancy rate (%)	Job vacancy rate in firms with job vacancies (%)	Average number of job vacancies in firms with job vacancies
≤20	0.1	4.5	1.2	25.5	1.8
20–99	0.2	9.1	0.6	6.1	2.5
100–499	1.7	23.1	0.7	3.2	7.3
≥500	10.8	38.6	0.7	1.7	28.0
Total	1.3	10.8	0.9	8.2	12.3

Very similar evidence to that measured in Table 1 for a specific reference period is found in all quarters.

Regarding the analysis of anomalous data, since the job vacancy distribution is sharply peaked on the zero, it is impossible in practice to identify true outliers among firms that declare to have no vacancies. However, in the presence of a relationship, even if weak, between vacancies and jobs, it has been possible to work out robust methods to identify outliers in the right side of the distribution (i.e. units with an anomalously large number of job vacancies) conditioned on the firm size.

In particular, outliers in the job vacancy variable are found as those units which do not fall inside given acceptance regions identified by robust regression techniques. Such techniques allow to avoid masking effects of anomalous values which can be found with more conventional estimators, such as ordinary least squares.

For job vacancies, the model, specified for the log of the ratio between vacancies and jobs, uses as regressors the log of jobs at the end of the quarter and dummy variables representative of the economic activity section. The parameters of the robust regression are estimated only on observations with non-zero job vacancies through Yohai's MM estimator (Yohai 1987), which combines a high breakdown value with good efficiency properties. Outliers are identified as those observations with regression residual larger than an empirically chosen threshold. In our case, the breakdown point level of the MM estimator has been set at 25 %, while the threshold for detecting outlying observations has been set to three times the scale. Observations identified as outliers are assigned an influence score which is used to discriminate between units candidates for selective or automatic editing. In both cases data are verified, for the first set of units through a recall of the firm, for the second set through the inspection of other auxiliary variables. If the observation is reputed to be valid it is kept, otherwise it is cancelled and passed to subsequent imputation procedures. In the latter case their impact on the final estimate is reduced.

Regarding the subsequent phase of the editing and imputation process, the imputation of non-responses, the following choice has been made: job vacancies are imputed both for the responding units with no response on the variable and for all the non-responding units belonging to the LES. In fact, for these firms information on jobs, hires, separations and hours worked is already available from the LES, and it can be used to impute the number of job vacancies. Moreover, job vacancies are also imputed when jobs are imputed, since in these cases it seems likely that the collected figures on both variables refer to a mis-identified sample unit (for example, only to a portion of the entire unit, or to a different one altogether).

As far as the imputation procedures are concerned, since the share of firms with job vacancies is another variable of interest, we have chosen job vacancy imputation methods which do not introduce a systematic error in its estimate. Since those such as mean (or conditioned mean) imputation always attribute strictly positive job vacancy values in all the cases where at least one responding firm in the class where the mean is calculated has at least a vacancy, they would tend to produce upwardly biased estimates of the share of firms with job vacancies. Therefore, we have chosen not to use them.

On the other side, because of the peculiarities of the job vacancy variable, it is difficult to specify parametric regression models for it. In particular, extensive analyses have been carried out on the possibility to use two-stage models, with a first stage represented by a logistic model distinguishing between firms with and without vacancies and a second stage by a linear one estimating the number of vacancies for the units identified in the first stage as looking for candidates to hire. However, the available explanatory variables (mainly, jobs and lagged values of job vacancy rates and hires rates, besides economic activity and size classification ones) have always been found to leave a very large share of the dependent variable variance unexplained. Therefore, we could not adopt them.

As a last remark, since the job vacancy distribution is sharply peaked around zero and since the duration of vacancies is variable (excluding those economic activity sectors characterised by a strong seasonality), it is also impossible to specify autoregressive methods which allow to distinguish real zero values from zero values which mask an inability of the firm to provide a value for job vacancies.

The choice thus has fallen on a hot-deck method based on nearest neighbour donor imputation[6], which allows not to significantly distort the job vacancies distribution. Moreover this method, being non-parametric, makes no hypothesis on the functional form of the relationships among variables.

This method has been used both for LES units and for non-LES units, the only difference being the matching variables used for donor imputation, since for the two sets of units different auxiliary ones are available.

For LES firms, the variables used in the distance function are: jobs at the end of the quarter, lagged job vacancy rates, lagged hiring rates, and lagged jobs' growth rates.

For non-LES firms, the variables used in the distance function are: jobs at the end of the quarter, and the job vacancy rates in the previous quarter and in the same quarter of the previous year. The lagged job vacancy rates are used also in order to take into account a possible persistence of vacancies.

---

[6] See Kalton and Kasprzyk (1982), or Chen and Shao (2000), for a review.

Table 2 Job vacancies imputation rates (number of firms and share of total number of firms, average over 2010)

	Firms with imputed job vacancies				Firms with job vacancies	Total of firms
	Non responding LES firms	Non response on job vacancies	Imputed jobs	Total		
Number of firms Share of	298	17	23	338	8,641	8,979
total number of firms (%)	3.3	0.2	0.3	3.8	96.2	100.0

Source ISTAT, Quarterly survey on job vacancies and hours worked (VELA)

Finally, a specific treatment has been reserved for the non-responding LES firms with at least 10,000 employees. In fact, each of them has peculiar characteristics which strongly distinguish it from other enterprises of similar size or economic activity. Therefore, for such units the possible set of donors could have features too different from the receiving units. Hence, it has been chosen to use, when possible, a time series model on the data of each concerned enterprise, with lagged job vacancy and hiring rates among the regressors.

It is to be noted that the imputation rates due to item non-response are usually very small (0.2 % of the responding units on average in 2010, see Table 2). Similarly small are the imputation rates for units in which job vacancies are imputed as a consequence of jobs imputation (0.3 %). As far as LES firms are concerned, since it has been chosen to impute job vacancies on all non-respondents the imputation rate is much higher (3.3 % on average in 2010).

4 Calibration

At the end of the imputation procedures, the set of microdata has no remaining missing data in the jobs and job vacancy variables in any of the records. These correspond to: all the respondents non-LES firms and all the LES units (due to imputation of unit non-responses for all the enterprises in this panel).

To correct for unit non-responses of non-LES sample units and to make the data collected on non-LES firms representative of the part of the reference population which does not belong to the LES panel, the responding non-LES firms are calibrated.[7]

Grossing up to a reference population is not very common in ISTAT short-term business surveys. In fact, usually their target parameters are changes, in particular changes in index numbers, and are more frequently estimated via comparisons of responses in the reference period and the same period of the previous year and corrections to take into account the non-responses.

---

[7] For the methodological bases for calibration estimation, see Deville and Särndal (1992).

The main reason to carry out a grossing up of the data collected by VELA is that the target parameters of the survey are not only changes. In particular, they include the job vacancy rate and the number of job vacancies.

As mentioned above, in the VELA survey, the responding non-LES firms are grossed up via calibration. The theoretical reference population for this procedure is made by all the enterprises with at least 10 employees in NACE Rev. 2 sections B-N which were active in the reference quarter, with the exception of those in the LES panel. This population is well represented by the set of microdata of the OROS survey for the reference quarter, which is therefore used to derive the calibration constraints, as mentioned above.

This choice is peculiar to the VELA survey. In fact, in general, ISTAT structural business surveys use the SBR to obtain a reference population for calibration. For this type of surveys, the SBR available when the calibration is carried out refers to the same year as the sample data. However, this would not be the case for VELA, or for short term business surveys in general, that would have to use an SBR version referring to a year preceding the period for which the sample data were collected by one or two years. Furthermore, calibration to an SBR would mean to use the same known totals for an entire year, that is for four or twelve successive short term survey waves.

The set of microdata of the OROS survey for a given quarter becomes available around 62 days after the end of the quarter itself. Hence, it can be used to produce data on job vacancies within 70 days after the end of the reference quarter, as requested by the relevant EU regulations. In this way, the aggregate job vacancy data are obtained via a calibration to a population which changes from quarter to quarter and refers to the same quarter as the sample data.

Besides the above discussed advantages, there are also some specific difficulties related to the use of the OROS microdata as calibration constraints. In particular, because the set of microdata for the reference quarter is affected by a very small percentage of nonresponses (due to firms which are late in filling in and transmitting their social contributions declarations to INPS), a correction of the known totals to compensate for it is applied (Ceccato et al. 2011). Furthermore, in a limited number of cases the OROS microdata on jobs are found to differ markedly from those collected by VELA for reasons which seem to be related to specific characteristics of the OROS source. This happens, for example, for firms where some workers do not work even for one hour during the month and receive a Wage Supplementation Fund (in Italian, Cassa Integrazione Guadagni) for their entire monthly working time, because these workers are paid no social contributions in the month and therefore are not included in the firm's social contributions declaration to INPS for that month. It also happens for non-agricultural firms where some workers nevertheless carry out a work which is classified as agricultural and therefore are paid social contributions accordingly and are not included in the firm's social contributions declaration to INPS on which the OROS microdata are based. The cases where these differences between OROS and VELA jobs are large enough to imply a different classification of the unit in the calibration cells are dealt with as stratum jumpers, with a method described in the following.

As already mentioned above, for the non-LES VELA respondents, the calibration is carried out using the quarterly average of monthly data on jobs, as measured by OROS, as the auxiliary variable. Therefore, this calibration procedure increases the capability of aggregate data on jobs produced by VELA to represent the actual figure for this variable, with respect to a calibration to the SBR. Furthermore, as mentioned above, it produces estimates of jobs based on VELA for the above defined population which are coherent with those produced for the same population by OROS. The known totals are calculated on this variable and on the above defined set of units, in classes based on economic activity and enterprise size.[8] Starting from 2010, the economic activity classes for calibration are based on NACE Rev. 2 divisions for sections from C to E, G and N, while they are based on sections B, F, and from H to M. The considered size classes are based on employees and are thus defined: 10–19, 20–99, at least 100. It has been mentioned that the set of target parameters of the survey includes not only changes but also levels. However, as for all short term surveys, also for VELA the purpose to produce time series consistent over time is a very relevant one. Currently, this aim is pursued: via the longitudinal nature of the sample, which ensures that the responding units in successive waves or in waves referring to the same quarter of successive years overlap substantially; and by introducing longitudinal elements in the editing and imputation procedures wherever possible. Moreover, also the choice of the calibration constraints works towards this aim. A further way to strengthen the consistency over time of time series would be to use also longitudinal calibration constraints. However, the attempts made so far at implementing this method have not been successful: in many cases the additional longitudinal constraints prevent the convergence of the iterative distance minimization algorithm which estimates the calibration weights. Nevertheless, we believe that in the context of future improvements to the current data processing methods, this possibility could be given further consideration.

The initial calibration weights are based on both inclusion probabilities and response rates.

The calibration is carried out using a generalized software purposely built by ISTAT, GENESEES (Pagliuca 2005), and adopting a truncated logarithmic distance function.

The calibration method just described is modified to reduce the impact on the aggregate data of the stratum jumpers. As mentioned above, these are the records where jobs measured by VELA and OROS are substantially different, and more specifically those where the VELA figure for jobs would imply a classification of the firm in a calibration cell different from that to which the unit is assigned on the basis of the OROS figure for the variable. If the figure collected by VELA is substantially larger than the OROS one, it is likely that the calibration based on the latter as auxiliary variable ends up giving an undesirably large weight to the firm, which thus can become too influential on the aggregate data. To avoid this outcome,

---

[8] The geographical area is not used to define calibration classes, because for firms with more than one local unit the collected data do not allow to identify to which local units the job vacancies measured at the firm level actually refer to.

a special treatment is reserved for these records. First of all, the firm is assigned to a calibration cell on the basis of the maximum between the figures for jobs as measured by VELA and OROS. Furthermore, after a first calibration, a second one is carried out starting from a different set of initial weights. The firms for which the distance between jobs according to the two sources, once calibrated, is larger than a threshold, both in levels and as a share of the section jobs total, are given a unit initial weight. All the other firms in the calibration cells where at least one firm is given a unit initial weight have their initial weights increased so as to keep the sum of initial weights of the cell constant. All the other firms keep their first calibration initial weights. A second calibration is then carried out starting from the just described new set of initial weights. The second calibration final weights for the firms with unit initial weight are lower than the first calibration ones. In this way, the influence of the stratum jumpers on the aggregate data is reduced.

After the second calibration, the entire set of microdata is obtained by adding to the records of the LES enterprises, each with unit grossing up weight, those of the calibrated enterprises, each with the weight calculated as just described.

The job vacancy rate estimator for each study domain is therefore calculated as follows:

$$jvr_h = \frac{\sum\limits_{i \in S_h} jv_i \cdot w_i}{\sum\limits_{i \in S_h} (jobs_i + jv_i) \cdot w_i} \tag{1}$$

where w_i, jv_i and $jobs_i$ are, respectively, the second calibration grossing up weight, the number of job vacancies and the number of jobs at the end of the reference quarter for the i-th unit. The sum is on the units of the sample S_h resulting from the integration and editing and imputation procedures for the h-th study domain.

5 Concluding Remarks

In this paper the main characteristics of the Italian quarterly survey on job vacancies and hours worked run by ISTAT have been described and analysed with a particular regard to the job vacancy variable and its treatment.

In particular we focussed on some peculiarities of the process of editing, imputation and estimation and especially on two phases. The first one is the integration with two ISTAT business surveys, LES and OROS, all over the editing and imputation process which allows to maximise the consistency of the indicators produced by the three sources. The second one is the calibration of the collected variables with an uncommon choice of the grossing up population: the whole population of enterprises with at least one employee taken from the administrative OROS survey updated to the reference quarter, rather than the official statistical business register. These two aspects in fact are those which characterise and differentiate most this survey with respect to other short-term business ones.

As part of a continuous process of reassessment of the data processing procedures in use, we are considering to improve in the near future some methodological aspects of the estimation process. In particular, we are thinking of revising the set of units which are calibrated and the calibration cells, to take into account the fact that some non-LES enterprises with at least 100 employees currently can end up with grossing-up weights which seem too large. Furthermore, we would like to re-consider the treatment of stratum jumpers, in particular of those which are due to a difference in the definition of jobs between VELA and OROS. Finally, we would like to explore more in depth the possibility to introduce longitudinal calibration constraints which would provide a better consistency of aggregated series over time.

Acknowledgments This paper builds on the work done in the last years at ISTAT on the quarterly survey on job vacancies and hours worked. Ciro Baldi, Luisa Cosentino, Annalisa Lucarelli, Gian Paolo Oneto, Luisa Picozzi, Fabio Rapiti, Leonello Tronti have all participated in it in different roles, degrees of responsibility and periods of time. We wish to express our gratitude to all of them. ISTAT bears no responsibility for the analysis or interpretation of the data. All usual disclaimers apply.

References

Bethel, J. (1989). Sample allocation in multivariate surveys. *Survey Methodology, 15*, 46–57.

Ceccato, F., Cimino, E., Congia, M. C., Pacini, S., Rapiti, F. M., & Tuzi, D. (2011). *I nuovi indicatori trimestrali delle retribuzioni lorde, oneri sociali e costo del lavoro della rilevazione Oros in base 2005 e Ateco 2007*. Mimeo, ISTAT.

Chen, J., & Shao, J. (2000). Nearest neighbor imputation for survey data. *Journal of Official Statistics, 16*, 113–131.

Deville, J. C., & Särndal, C. E. (1992). Calibration estimators in survey sampling. *Journal of the American Statistical Association, 87*, 367–382.

Di Giuseppe, R., Giaquinto, P., & Pagliuca, D. (2004). *MAUSS (Multivariate allocation of units in sampling surveys): un software generalizzato per risolvere il problema dell'allocazione campionaria nelle indagini ISTAT*. Contributi 7.

Kalton, G., & Kasprzyk, D. (1982). Imputing for missing survey responses. In *Proceedings of the Section on Survey Research Methods* (pp. 22–31). American Statistical Association.

Pagliuca, D. (Ed.). (2005). *GENESEES v. 3.0 Funzione Riponderazione. Manuale utente ed aspetti metodologici*. Tecniche e Strumenti 2, ISTAT.

Thompson, K. J., & Sigman, R. S. (1996). Statistical methods for developing ratio edit tolerances for economic data. *Journal of Official Statistics, 15*, 517–535.

Yohai, V. J. (1987). High breakdown-point and high efficiency robust estimates for regression. *The Annals of Statistics, 15*, 642–656.

About the Authors

Tomás Aluja-Banet is a professor of statistics and data analysis of the Universitat Politécnica de Catalunya–Barcelona Tech (UPC) (Spain) since 1983. His research interests include methodological aspects of multivariate analysis, segmentation trees, data fusion, and PLS path models, with their software implementation. He is coordinator of the European Master on Data Mining and Knowledge Management.

Caterina Arcidiacono is a full professor of Social and Community Psychology. Coordinator of the Ph.D. School in Relational and Pedagogical Sciences, and Coordinator of the Ph.D. Course in Gender Studies, at the Federico II University of Naples (Italy). She is Director of INCOPARDE Lab. (www.incoparde.unina.it) and president of European Community Psychology Association (ECPA).

Simona Balbi is a full professor in Statistics, University of Naples Federico II. Her research interests are multivariate descriptive data analysis, and textual data analysis, especially in relation with Text Mining. She is editor of Sage series "Research Methods for Social Scientists" (with J. Blasius, C. van Dijkum, A. Ryen) and coeditor of the *Italian Journal of Applied Statistics*.

Diego Bellisai is a researcher at Istat, the Italian national statistical office, where he works on short-term statistics on labour input. He holds a Ph.D. in Theoretical Physics and his research interests are related in particular to methods of editing and imputation in business surveys.

Luigi Biggeri is a professor emeritus of Economic Statistics at the University of Florence and Fellow of the American Statistical Association. He has been president of Italian National Institute of Statistics (2001–2009) and president elect of the International Association of Survey Statisticians (2003–2005).

Josep Daunis-i-Estadella is a professor at the Department of Computer Science and Applied Mathematics, the University of Girona. He studied Mathematics at the University Autonoma of Barcelona and obtained his Ph.D. from the UPC in

C. Davino and L. Fabbris (eds.), *Survey Data Collection and Integration*,
DOI: 10.1007/978-3-642-21308-3, © Springer-Verlag Berlin Heidelberg 2013

Barcelona (2005). His main research topics since then has been the fusion methods and the statistical analysis of compositional data.

Cristina Davino is an associate professor in Statistics at the University of Macerata, Italy. Her research fields include: multidimensional data analysis, data mining (neural networks, association rules), quantile regression, statistical surveys, sensitivity analysis of composite indicators, evaluation of quality of life, and evaluation of educational planning.

Immacolata Di Napoli has a Ph.D. in Psychological and pedagogical sciences, she is a psychologist and teaches community psychology at Federico II, University in Naples (Italy). She has carried out researches in the field of social and community psychology, investigating the dimensions correlated to a sense of community, belonging, sense of power, and the expectation on personal and collective planning in local contexts.

Luigi Fabbris is a full professor in Social Statistics at the Statistics Department, the University of Padua, Italy, where he lectures in Survey Methodology and Social Statistics. His research fields are multivariate analysis, survey sampling, and questionnaire design; he was also active in social indicators, nexuses between education and work, social conditions of women, immigrants, the elderly, and the homeless.

Stefania Fivizzani is a researcher at Istat, the Italian national statistical office, where she works on short-term statistics on labor input. Her research interests are related in particular to business surveys organizational aspects.

Caterina Giusti is a researcher in Statistics at the Department of Statistics and Mathematics Applied to Economics of the University of Pisa. Ph.D. in Applied Statistics at the University of Florence in 2008. Her research interests include multilevel models, imputation for nonresponses in sample surveys, small area estimation models.

Yan Hong Chen is a statistician, working in the Statistical Institute of Catalonia (Idescat) since 2006 in the Department of Specialist Statistical Assistance Area. He gives technical support on statistics subjects inside the Institute and any other Catalan government department. His job is focused on data fusion and small area estimation, missing data, sample survey, and survey data calibration using Calmar.

Stefano Marchetti is a researcher in Statistics at the Department of Statistics and Mathematics Applied to Economics, University of Pisa. He holds a Ph.D. in Applied Statistics from the Department of Statistics, University of Florence (2009). He has research interests in survey sampling methodology, resampling methods, small area estimation, with special focus on M-quantile models, and on poverty mapping.

Monica Pratesi is an associate professor in Statistics at Pisa University. Her main research fields include small area estimation and inference from survey data. She coordinates the Sample Survey Group of the Italian Statistical Society and coordinated a collaborative project on Small area Methodologies for Poverty and Living Conditions Estimates (S.A.M.P.L.E.) funded by the European Commission in the 7th Framework Program.

Rosaria Romano is a researcher in Statistics at the University of Calabria, Department of Economy and Statistics. She has been involved in many national and international projects. Her most important publications are related to the fields of methodological statistics and applied statistics with focus on sensory and consumer science.

Marina Sorrentino is a researcher at Istat, the Italian national statistical office, where she works on short-term statistics on labor input. She has experience of analysis of historical data and has been a consultant for projects aimed at the harmonisation of statistical systems and the World Bank.

Nicole Triunfo graduated in business administration and management, she is a Ph.D. student in Statistics at University of Naples Federico II, Department of Mathematics and Statistics. Her main research fields include textual data analysis, information extraction, official statistics, text categorisation.